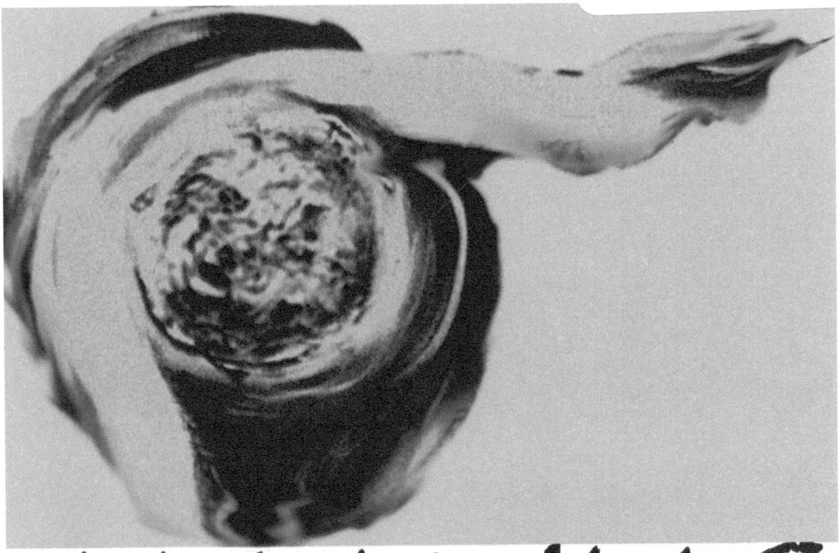

AMAZING
anthology

Published by the Antelope Valley Writers Association
Palmdale, CA 93551

Please visit our website: http://avwritersassociation.wordpress.com

Front cover artwork, *Creation* © Patricia Alexander
Front cover design by Doreen Kennedy

ISBN: 978-0-692-34297-8

DEDICATION

This book is dedicated to Dave R. Ostman and Gary D. Burgess, former members of the Antelope Valley Writers Association. They were two men who were devoted to their families and their Antelope Valley communities, two men so different yet so alike. Both were talented writers who left us this past year all too soon. They are truly missed but will forever inspire us with their stories and poetry, which are featured in this anthology.

The anthology title, *AMAZING*, came to be after reading Dave's poem "Amazing" which is featured on Page 18.

About the ANTELOPE VALLEY WRITERS ASSOCIATION

The Antelope Valley Writers Association (AVWA) is a non-profit literary group that is free and open to the adult public. Their primary belief is that everyone has a story to tell; that every person is a walking storybook full of wisdom, history, and imagination.

AVWA members are everyday people who live in the amazing high desert of the Antelope Valley. Among them are doctors, teachers, students, artists, business owners, librarians, executive assistants, salespersons, counselors, aerospace employees, homemakers, firemen, ministers, and even a former Las Vegas showgirl. All have a love of writing and a desire to share their stories. In fact, the group's motto is, "Words are meant to be shared," and that's exactly what these talented individuals do at weekly meetings and in their anthologies.

In 2013 the AVWA published its first anthology, *Soaring*, a collection of short stories, poems, and memoirs written by members of the group. Copies of *Soaring* are available through the group or from Amazon.com. The success of *Soaring* led to a second book, *AMAZING*, and started an annual tradition of AVWA anthologies. With the publication of *AMAZING* the AVWA continues its support for local students by dedicating funds from the sales of its anthologies to provide scholarships through the Antelope Valley College Foundation.

About the *AMAZING* anthology

This is the AVWA's second anthology. It differs from their first, *Soaring*, in two ways: (1) it has an inspirational theme as a tribute to two proficient members of the group who passed in 2014, and (2) submissions were open to all writers who reside in the Antelope Valley. The high desert is indeed a place for the arts as thirty-three talented wordsmiths, from middle-school students to retirees, are included in *AMAZING*.

ACKNOWLEDGMENTS

The AVWA would like to thank the following people whose hard work and dedication made this anthology a reality:

- Patricia Alexander, an amazing artist as well as a talented writer, for allowing her painting, *Creation*, to grace the cover, for chairing our weekly meetings, and for being the ideal hostess – always there with a beautiful smile.

- Doreen Kennedy, the anthology project manager, for taking on the huge tasks of collecting, editing, formatting, and publishing the anthology.

- Dennis Anderson, editor of the Antelope Valley Press award winning local newspaper, for always providing support for the AVWA and the Antelope Valley communities in general.

- and the literati of the Antelope Valley, inspired and ever amazed by the beauty of the high desert. May you continue to grow, prosper, and write.

About the COVER and ARTIST:

Patricia Alexander, a visual artist and writer born in Buffalo, New York, currently lives in Lancaster, California. Her artwork has been shown throughout the United States as well as in Italy, France, and the former Yugoslavia. Some of her art has also been published in magazines and books, and in specialty publications such as *Art Buzz*.

Pat creates an uncanny vibrancy in her abstract paintings as well as those in her favorite style, magic realism, with a focus on carnival life. Her colorful and intense abstract, entitled *Creation*, is featured on the cover. A poem of the same title, written by Pat and inspired by her painting, can be found on Page 44.

CONTENTS

DAVE R. OSTMAN 12
  Hesitation 12
  A.V. Poetry 13
  True Love 14
  The Eye of the Hare 15
  My Oak Tree 16
  Someday, It Will Be Her She Sees 16
  Parables in Perception 17
  Amazing 18
  Never 19
GARY D. BURGESS 20
  For Shirley 20
  Be Kind, Rewind 21
  Friends 22
  The Vote That Counts 23
  He Wasn't 24
  Different Measures of Time 25
  Today Is the First Day 26
  A Dream In My Pocket 27
ALICE HUDSON 28
  Ode to Rain 28
  Colosseum Story 29
  I Love Horses, But Sometimes They Don't Like Me 30
  Are You All Crazy?! 31
  Recollections of the Greatest Generation 33
DOROTHY BACHELOR 34
  An Event In My Life 34
PAT ALEXANDER 37
  God's Face 37
  Baby Otto 38
  Full Moon 40
  Winter In Antelope Valley 41
  Lancaster Boulevard 42
  Creation 44
ESPERANZA BELTRAN 45
  Sliding Into Fear 45

JACKIE L. CROSSWHITE SR. 51
Coo-Coo Bird 51
Staring 51
Around the World 51
My Guardian Angels 52
I Am a Winner 54
Searching for Anything 56
Offend 57
Once 57
Share 57
Lookout 57
Live ItUp 57
MIA LEE 58
My Thanksgiving Day 58
GINA HUDGENS 62
Inspired 62
Will You 63
A Girls' Night Out 64
My Song Bird 65
Fullfillment 66
Kindness 66
G.I.G.G.L.E.S 67
PATRICIA CURRAN LOVE 68
Christmas in August 68
CHRISTOPHER E. LOVE 70
Ernie and Casper 70
Goodbye to the Fisherman 73
MARY DENNING 78
The Morning Light 78
Sea Shells and Roller Skates 79
Barney Google 80
Angels in Our Lives 81
Hands 82
Soaring 83
Watermelon Wine 84
A Mother's Love 85
KATIE RYAN 86
The Month of May 86
The Soldier 88

STEVE ORDWAY

    Sitting on Go – Life at the Fire Factory 89

    Close Call 92

    Chihuahua 94

    Happy Chief 95

ELAINE BROWN 96

    Silver Queen 96

    Ice Fantasy 96

    Rose Garden 96

    Moonlit Garden 96

    Summers in Canada 97

    The Spirit of Kauai 101

MELINDA M. HUNTER 103

    Rain 103

    Spring 104

    October's Voice 105

    Laroes to Catch Meddlers 106

    What Christmas Means to Me 107

LOIS WILK 108

    Memorable Moments, Sounds of Silence 108

    The Cake 110

    Honnniee, Honniee 111

LA RUE ALEGRIA 112

    Here Comes the Bride 112

    Fall 114

    Carpe Diem 115

    The Adobe 116

    The Starry Host 118

    Guardian Angel 119

ERIKA HAWKINS 120

    Like Mind 120

    An Ant's Survival 121

    Chicken Soup 122

RICHARD C. ELTON, M.D. 123

    Tide Pools 123

    A Light in the Sky 124

    The Speeding Ticket 125

    The Rummage Sale 126

    Ode to the Spider 127

The Journal in My Mind...128
Father's Day 129
WILMA P. WEBSTER..130
Deployed!..130
Rock Garden 133
Loos Around the World 135
LEMOZINE RIDDICK...138
Stepping Out 138
MICHELE ELISE PADILLA 140
Time/Life 140
Blue Moon Friend 141
Dog Walk...141
That's My Boy...142
Baby Ballerina 143
JOYCE SANDERSON...144
Life Is Love Full of Reason 144
In the Middle of a Storm...145
MARILYN DALRYMPLE...146
The Great Equalizer..146
Help Comes in All Shapes and Sizes 148
ADRIANA ALEXANDER 150
Love Is Constant 150
Glimmers of You 151
No One Is Ever Alone...152
The Broadway Market 153
STEVEN BRITO 155
One Day...155
EKENE UGOCHUKWU...156
Mom and Daughter..156
Amazing America...157
The Orphan..158
MMELI UGOCHUKWU..159
Don't Close the Book..159
Election..160
AUDREY VANDENBERG..161
Naming 161
Mikasa 162
Ms. Mata Endlessly 163

TRISHA PRITCHARD..164
   The Unwilling Choice 164
   Don't Talk To Me About It..168
KIT BENNETT 170
   Significance of a Stranger's Smile.................................170
KATHY ANDREWS...172
   Mojave Desert Magic 172
OLEG KAGAN 175
   4 Haiku..175
   Small Household Pet..176
   In the Museum Courtyard 176
DOREEN KENNEDY 177
   Life Debt..177

Individual Copyrights 185

The Antelope Valley Writers Association
thanks you for your support,
and hopes that you enjoy the poetry and prose
of the many talented residents of
the Antelope Valley.

DAVE R. OSTMAN

Dave R. Ostman, a native of Ohio, was a talented poet, writer, and humanitarian who resided in Littlerock, California, within the Antelope Valley. Before focusing on his literary pursuits and many volunteer efforts helping veterans and the homeless, Dave was an aerospace Flight Test and Delivery Manager, a Human Resources Manager, and a local businessman, as well as a father to five children. His writings have received honorable mention in a number of local and national competitions including runner-up in the Antelope Valley "Walk On Words" poetry contest. His poem "Amazing" inspired the title for this anthology.

A prolific poet and a philosopher by nature, Dave was also an avid playwright, completing two plays. His final project, mainly set in a homeless shelter, is a reflection of his writing and life philosophy: to focus in a common way on the perceptions we all share. Dave, who preferred to use just his initials DRO, is a talent truly missed.

HESITATION

With hesitation, I touch the pen to page.
Confusion abounds as to what to say,
Who, What, Where,
shall I write about today?
Words and subjects all knotted up;
like a child's tangled kite that just won't fly.

Focus, focus, instead questions,
much like a cup half-full, with confused expectations.
Where do I start and where do I end.
I knew before I started, it was all in my head.

Why won't it just roll down and magically overtake my fingers
to say what I mean to say, in pigment on page;
something that may be lost forever,
if I can't write what I want to say.

A treasure lost forever, in the dark and distant caverns,
of my unsure and hesitating mind!

A.V. POETRY

Bold this statement I am about to make within this song of words,
This muse from a valley of rare antelope and mystical jackalopes;
Where poppies range from white to lilac, then gold, a blush of red;
Lush landscapes in the spring
    and a valley where tall fans capture the wind each day,
From the breeze which shapes this sand.

Yuccas and palm trees mingle in this maze called the Antelope Valley,
Where nomads from all corners of the globe, set down their roots.
Hot, cold and unforgiving but proud to be called a High Desert Rat
    for those who choose to call, the A.V. their home.
A rare jewel, that sets in the shadows,
of the San Gabriel's, and the Tehachapi's.

This gateway to the city of angels,
Opal in luster this gemstone of white, black, red, brown, and yellow,
A hidden mine of riches
From a multiplicity of cultures and theologies.

Home of the quest, to search in further heavens,
Born from the shuttle now launch pad to space dreamers.
X-1 and after, all statements to a national treasure;
Green future in a valley still known, for antelopes and jackalopes.

Reveille broken by the buzz of the Mojave green
As it warns an errant roadrunner of desert shades
That its presence has been made
And that all about, must now become afraid.

If there is any flavor that this valley of the antelope does offer,
It is the sky especially at sunset where this valley is repainted anew.
Blues, and purple majesty set with orange and rose hues
Adorned by clouds, embrace each prism inside a separate rainbow.

Home, this homogony of progress where new ideas are born
And old stubborn ways are one day set down.
Born yet segregated, two communities in concert to become the icon,
There is a way to partner, for a mutual and strategic future.
As a muse sings, a muse dreams the same dream,
A dream that has brought so many souls to this valley.
This slice of Eden, called the High Desert.

TRUE LOVE

Bond between Child and Mother, none stronger;
Nine months and then always and forever.
Conceiving to create life; the artist pales in her shadow.
Love knows no stronger.

Always to know, learned when an infant,
You to her are more important than she
But always to be known, you are her creation.

A mingling of atoms from Mother and Father, this person you are
A soup made from a recipe of your heritage,
Blending to become the personality called you.

No bond ever stronger than a Mother who gave life to one so fragile
Days and nights of endless hardships are forgotten
When she drinks your beauty, through eyes of amazement.
Cradling you in arms with soothing whispers,
You know it is safe to close your eyes
The guardian who bore you will stand vigil
As you play in the dreams of your innocence,
Surrounded by a love that has no equal.

THE EYE OF THE HARE

One day long ago I looked deep into the eyes of a young rabbit
which was trapped half-way inside a link of chain fencing.
Natural instinct took over,
without hesitation I spoke to this frightened creature.
As I gently took him into my hands to extract him from his prison,
didn't know boy or girl, just little and scared
with a heartbeat faster than a hummingbird's wings.

Still whispering to sooth,
remarkably I was able to manipulate that tiny body
out of his tiny cell without injury.
I held this gift from the heavens in my hands,
lightly touching the back of its head
and feeling his heartbeat settle down
to a normal rhythm of beat.

As I sat him back down to hop away,
he paused to look directly into my eyes.

I felt his aura of thankfulness surround me,
I knew that the Universe had touched me
with the Eye of the Hare and the Heart of the Rabbit.
A memory,
when the heavens, united the spirits, of two so different souls.

MY OAK TREE

Another summer day, soon scorching, with dragonflies
Skimming over a sky-blue lake;
And there a pair of osprey,
Dancing together in flight, at the most unbelievable height.

A lagoon of indigo blue, under an old oak tree
provides comfort as I watch
Cautious fish dart to avoid a possible mistake, at the hungry talons
that could
Foretell their fates.

My old oak tree is far older than me – centuries I think its time
– mine a blink.
As I drink in the beauty that the universe now shares with me,
I can't but pause to admire what has been given to us,
To preserve and protect including each and every soul
That dreams, to adopt an old oak tree
Like me.

SOMEDAY, IT WILL BE HER SHE SEES

Young dreamer on an empty stage;
For many years ahead from today will be her day,
but a young aspirant bride from today still to dream.
No Prince today, for that day, she still cannot see.

Now empty, the stage from any marriage ceremony,
where the child woman dreams of that someday
when it will be her.
What life lies ahead for her from this moment
when mesmerized the dream struck
and she committed that she too would be the Bride,
this perpetual dream
till that someday, it will be, her she sees.

PARABLES IN PERCEPTION

Perceptions influencing our decisions should demand examination.
Approaching
perceptions without pre-judgment must meet the criteria.

Awareness and understanding in the art of listening,
then begin to condition, the ease of perception.

Whether
the complexity of design, forming the wings of a monarch butterfly
or
the reflection of moonlight across an autumn pond,
perceptions affect each of us alike and differently,
based on our histories and our ability in the art of awareness.

Is it true
that the Mona Lisa smiles or that Mount Everest is really so high?
Does she or he really love me,
or is it just a mistake in my mind's eye?

Learning to listen and be open is a challenging prescription
when one takes the time to improve their perceptions.

A parable in time and improvement must be common,
if one is committed to learn the truth,
behind what we call our perceptions.

AMAZING

This life we taste, from sweet to bitter.

Amazing

This birth, then death.
Each of us with our own clock of time.
The blink of an eye;
each our own glimpse of life.

Amazing

This union of molecules we call human.
Magic from the Cosmos, Creation from the Stars, but mere mortal;
Our fate sealed, that perhaps someday our souls will fly together,
Until some unknown day.

Amazing

This Celestial puzzle.
This Maze of emotions and experiences passes, while our lives fly by.
Dead-end, detour, turned around, never a perfect score.
Yet those before us bequeath that the living light the candle of hope,
Which will help unite tomorrow's children, into an army of love.

If we could only but teach the future, by the mistakes from the past,
We would make an incredible contribution
to our world, our cosmos,
and to our universe
and thus, become even more

Amazing.

NEVER

Addictive this persuasion that drags my heart to regurgitate,
  words with such emotion.

            To stop? Ohhh – no, no never.

Like a drummer who beats the skin of spirits
Thunder cascades and clouds of words and sound surround;
A sky of golden butterflies.
Cerebral, elliptical, streaking then careening,
To pause, to float as tender feathers, words, in the fragile air.

            Stop? Ohhh – no, no never.

Break my fingers, I'll find a way.
Break my heart and I'll pour what's left of my blood
  into a last, sad love song.
My task, to pluck the words before lost, as they quickly
  dance and pass my way.
Not ego, the fire which consumes but instead the demand of others
That these magical butterflies must be caught.
Delicately I pin them to the page, at times in no particular order.
Thousands of words now grace my palette.

            Now should I stop? Ohhh – no, no never.

Still they fly about my mind, like bees inside my bonnet head.
Familiar bond, with those who share this common addiction;
Buzz becomes roar, hand begins to tremble, a new ensemble tuning;
Now a frantic search to find a way to save it.

            Stop? – Ohhh – no, no never.

A platypus with pink ponytails just went by,
Followed by a fellow named Dante, seemingly lost in an Inferno.
Einstein said, "Imagination is more important than knowledge."
Inside all, resides a golden bird that needs to fly
Amongst the world, of golden words,
  much like the gold, inside my stately butterflies.
Yes – My Passion – Forever!

            Stop? – Ohhh – No, No Never!

GARY D. BURGESS

Gary Burgess, born in West Virginia, spent most of his life in Lancaster, California. He was an aircraft electrician in the U.S Air Force and later worked on the Mercury and Gemini space capsules in Florida. His transfer to Edwards Air Force Base began a 42 year love affair with the Antelope Valley where he managed to combine work, family, personal life, and civic activism. A tireless community advocate, he helped bring about improvements to the local Piute neighborhood where a street was named in his honor.

Gary's personal life was full of adventure: racing cars, flying hot air balloons, camping, fishing, skiing, distance riding on his bike, and, of course, writing. Gary enjoyed writing about his personal passions: his family, friends, the simple things of life, and most of all his wife of 54 years, Shirley, his childhood sweetheart.

FOR SHIRLEY

If I could be one thing for you…
It would be a daisy…

And as you would pick the petals from me,
  It wouldn't be
    "He loves me,
      He loves me not"

Every one of the endless petals
that make up my physical presence
Would cry out as you picked them

"He loves me!
  He loves me!
    He loves me!…"

Gary D. Burgess

BE KIND, REWIND

When I was young
A radio we had
For entertainment or news
Sometimes happy, sometimes sad

Over the years
More devices came about
Telephones to talk to friends
GPS gadgets to map our route

We now have cell phones and PC's
We can send text messages and such
We need all these things
Because these days we are in such a rush

Sometimes we need to put these things aside
Take our grandchild by the hand
Get the fishing poles and bologna sandwiches
Dig up some worms and put them in a can

Rewind back to a simpler time
Looking at life through the eyes of a six year old
Remember when life was simpler for us
No need for that cell phone, just to be put on hold

Spend an afternoon with that grandchild
Tell stories about your life
Share what they are interested in
Tell them how you met your wife

Tell them about their grandma
How she loved and cared for their mother
Tell of all you shared over the years
And that you had never loved another

Just maybe this sharing
Will impart a spark of knowledge
Your grandchild will grow older
Learn something that isn't taught in college

Before it's too late in your life
Be kind, rewind
Share with those you love a part of your life
When you laughed, loved, and lived in a simpler time

FRIENDS

A friend is someone who tries to understand
Even when there is no obvious explanation

A friend is someone who hurts because you hurt
And feels good when you feel good

A friend is someone who accepts you the way you are
And doesn't try to mold you into the way they want you to be

A friend is someone who will be there to help when you
Call on them

A friend is someone who will give to you and ask
Nothing in return

A friend is someone who will never forget the good
times you've had together and will let the memory of the
bad times fade as time passes

A friend is someone who will try to nourish and
enhance the friendship by responding whenever the time
comes that you call and say "I need you"

As in the past, and in the future

I call you friend

THE VOTE THAT COUNTS

The Orgas Grade School served not only as a building for the teaching of 1st through 5th grades, but as a polling place as well. When I attended school there, the school house consisted of only three rooms. If my memory serves me right, 1st and 2nd grade were in one room, 3rd and 4th grade in the middle room, and the 5th grade in a room by itself.

During the war years, I remember the piles of metal out by the hard road. We would gather any and all pieces of scrap metal and bring it to school to add to the pile.

I also remember going with my father to the school house so he could vote on Election Day. I'd watch the men talk and occasionally play with a schoolmate. On this particular day I noticed my father talking to one of the men who was running for office. I followed them around the corner of the schoolhouse, wondering where they were going as they moved away from the crowd gathered out front. I saw the candidate pass a small bottle to my father who placed it in his rear pocket. After my father finished his conversation with this gentleman they walked back to the front of the building, shook hands, and parted ways. Later on, this same scene played out with another candidate and again I followed them around to the back of the building. This time I saw what I thought was a dollar bill exchange hands.

When we got home that afternoon, I listened in on some of the conversation between my mother and father:

Mom: "Where did you get the whiskey?"

Dad: Oh, you know John who is running for County Sheriff. He was passing out a little enticement to get votes."

Mom: "And the two dollar bill?"

Dad: "Well Alfred who is also running for County Sheriff, he was buying votes."

Mom: "But you can only vote for one. Why did you promise both men you would vote for them?"

Dad: "Will I didn't really promise either one that I would vote for him, and neither one will know who I really voted for. And that is the great thing about a secret ballot."

HE WASN'T

He wasn't a man of great stature or
Of power, fame and fortune.
To look at him he didn't look very strong at all.

He wasn't someone who spoke to tell you
Of his accomplishments, his dreams or ambitions.
These he carried inside, as private possessions.

He wasn't someone who complained often at all.
Very seldom did he voice his displeasure out loud,
But when he spoke, he wasn't easily ignored.

He wasn't someone who took marriage vows lightly.
Loving someone during the good times is easy,
It was the times of struggle that made him stand tall among men.

He wasn't a Father that was afraid to give
Whether it was a gift, bought by the sweat of his brow,
Or the punishment that was for the well being of all involved.

He wasn't just another working man
Putting in his hours for a meager day's pay,
He gave his heart and soul to the job for those eight hours.

He wasn't one to shirk his responsibilities
Be it his Family, Job, or Church.
A handshake or his word was his commitment.

Others can remember their fathers for what they were;
I'm glad that I remember my Father
For what he wasn't.

DIFFERENT MEASURES OF TIME

It took me YEARS to truly fall in love with you.
To know you well enough to realized that
Without you I am an incomplete person.

In the past it may have taken MONTHS for me to realize
what a wonderful Mother you are. After watching our children
mature with your guidance, I know now how fortunate I
have been that you were the Mother of my children.

Sometimes DAYS would pass before I would say "I love you," and
for each time that happened, I'm truly sorry I let that opportunity slip
by.

Forgive me for the times that I wasted HOURS before apologizing to
you for what I had said or done to hurt you.

Wanting to say just the right words, at times I have pondered
MINUTES before telling you what I had to say, as I have tried to
comfort you in times of sadness.

I cherish each SECOND that I can spend with you. When I hold you
close, I feel not only a physical closeness with our bodies, but also
with our hearts.

TODAY IS THE FIRST DAY

Today is the first day
of the rest of my life
What will I do to make it
the best for me and my wife

Will I handle it better
when things go wrong
Accept that which I cannot change
to carry on with a song

Will I compliment
and give praise
To those I deal with
Throughout the days

Will I choose to care
by helping my fellow man
Remembering those less fortunate
in many a different land

Will I tell my loved ones
how much they mean to me
Remembering to carry a smile
so that others might see

Will I let my grandchildren
know of our family's past
So they can cherish their heritage
with good memories that will last

Will I set goals for myself
that are realistic and worthwhile
Remembering my age and limitations
Handling life inch by inch instead of by the mile

Will I let my wife know
how much she means to me
Cherishing each moment together
with a caring love, the way it should be

Will I try throughout the day
to cause no harm and not deceive
To help others in their struggles
to hold fast in what I believe

Yes I will, I tell myself
I choose to do these things and more
I choose to live today
by accepting what life has in store.

A DREAM IN MY POCKET

I've tried hard
Really I have
I worked to provide for my family
And tried to save to be rich

I've lived my life for enjoyment
To love my family
No one but someone like me knows the aspirations of a poor boy
To have more and to be well off

But I must say, I've had friends
More than a few
Lots of times those friends have been with me
As we escaped some of life's catastrophes

If I die poor, then let it be
If I die while trying to accomplish something, then let it be
If I die doing what I want, then let it be
Just let me die with a dream in my pocket, that's me
Never giving up.

ALICE HUDSON

Alice Hudson is a native Californian and a graduate of Chapman University. She has resided in several West Coast locations but now calls the Antelope Valley her home. Her various adventures, humorous experiences, and passionate interest in amateur stage and the arts have formed the basis for her yearning to write about laughter and life. She and her husband have been married for 54 years and have owned and operated a Hallmark store for 26 years, which contributes even more material for her writing. Alice loves to laugh as does her family - a daughter, son-in-law, and two grandsons. She hopes her writing has and will continue to capture the humor and laughter which has been so important to her.

ODE TO RAIN

I love rain.
It keeps me sane.

Whether downpour or drizzle
Rain makes my day sizzle.

Flowers drink in life's nectar
While people curse "ah hector."

Too much or too little
Creates lives a bit brittle.

The joy of a downpour
Opens heaven's door.

Walking in the rain is a treasure
Like our talking – pure pleasure.

So here's to rain
Long may it reign!

Alice Hudson

COLOSSEUM STORY

"The Colosseum has stood for almost 2000 years; we hope it's good for another few minutes." So spoke Roger, the eternal optimist, as we pressed ourselves against the outer walls of Rome's famous Colosseum. A sudden wind-driven rainstorm soaked us, scattered souvenirs, and broke glass from the kiosks around the plaza. All we five wanted to do was buy a few books to take home to the grandchildren. The bookstalls had disappeared. In their place, enterprising vendors switched to selling umbrellas, only five euro each. The four of us crowded under one umbrella as my daughter was invited to share one with some Londoners who were also backed up to the Colosseum walls.

The rest of our tour group, all twenty-eight of them, were nowhere to be seen. Obviously they had returned to the bus with our fearless bus driver, Pepe. On the other hand, our Roman tour guide was a dud, instructing Pepe to drive on without us. Two of the group had tried to locate us to show us the way to the bus, but were turned back by the weather just one entrance short of where we were huddled.

Never underestimate an Italian bus driver! Pepe ignored the guide and proceeded to drive the streets on the perimeter of the Colosseum. Watching for our bus, we counted several tour company busses similar to ours. The motto of the day was, "Watch for Pepe."

Never in the annals of touring has a sweeter sight been seen than that by five soaking wet Californians – it was Pepe, our hero! He chanced stopping on a busy highway where he should not have. Our travel pals had spotted us and were waving their arms frantically from inside the bus. If you've never hurried across slick, wet Roman marble walkways and streets, you haven't experienced tricky!

Roger again voiced our thoughts, "Pepe will definitely receive a heck of a good tip for this." Of course, no tip for what's-her-face, the Roman tour guide. To this day, we toast Pepe with glasses of, what else, Italian wine.

I LOVE HORSES, BUT SOMETIMES THEY DON'T LIKE ME

In order to show off in front of my future husband's family, I mounted Buck. I should have known what was in store from a name like that! He took off at a full gallop and made a sharp left turn at the wooden bridge over an irrigation ditch. I flew off and over the side of the bridge, narrowly missing a vertical upright, and landed head first in the ditch. I carry the dent on my head to this day. I love horses, but sometimes they don't like me.

One summer my husband and I, together with our buddies Barbara and Bob, spent time in Mammoth Lakes, California. We decided to take a full day horseback ride offered by the local stables. Barbara, being a bit skeptical of the ride, decided to stay behind to finish her book. Smart move!

The three of us boarded our horses at the Lake Mary stables and rode through magnificent trees and lovely creeks. Our destination, Duck Lake, was at the end of a ride out of the Mammoth Lakes basin and over a rocky divide where we had our box lunch and did some successful fishing. Now let me explain that being 4' 11" tall at the time, I was aboard a regulation sized horse with the stirrups set about as short as possible, and my legs were spread far apart due to the horse's girth. I rode this way for the entire ride. And it had been several years since I had ridden a horse.

At the end of the day's ride, with help from a wrangler, I dismounted and kept thinking the ground simply had to be there, somewhere. Finally my toes hit the ground and I let go of the saddle. Wrong move! I simply could not straighten up as my legs had been in the widespread position for the duration of the ride. Of course, my husband and Bob nearly collapsed with laughter at the sight of me all hunched over and barely able to stand. However, they did grab me, one on each side, and assisted me to our vehicle. It was also at that point when I realized my plan of joining the annual four day trail ride from the stables to the lower elevation winter range was not going to happen. I kept thinking Barbara would say, "Told ya – get a book, not a horse."

ARE YOU ALL CRAZY?!

"Are you all crazy?!" So questioned our children when the six of us told them we planned on "vacationing" in the high Sierras by backpacking from Yosemite to Mammoth.

The year was 1981. Our group consisted of one individual over fifty, the rest in their forties. For the month prior to our walk, we met after work and shrugged on backpacks filled with heavy objects, then walked the neighborhoods of Lancaster to prepare for our adventure. Dogs barked and children stared.

But we were ready as we were dropped off in Tuolumne Meadows. "Pick us up in four days at the Mammoth ski lodge at 2:45 PM," my husband announced (he is extremely sharp when it comes to time schedules).

Have you ever encountered switch-backs? A switch-back is a trail that zigzags up an incline that is too steep to travel straight up. Well our first day on the combined Pacific Crest and John Muir trail was nothing but switch-backs. We camped the first evening near a troop of Boy Scouts who warned us that they would blow whistles if bears were sighted near camp. Sure enough, at daybreak the next morning we heard whistles. One of our group was relieving himself as the bear ambled by; another tried to put his pants on in his sleeping bag – totally impossible. He wanted to get out of his tent to take pictures of the bear. His wife told him it wouldn't make any difference to the bear if he had his pants on.

That day was quite difficult as we scaled the 11,056 foot Donahue Pass. Do not ever believe oncoming hikers coming DOWN the trail. If I ever hear, "It's a piece of cake," again, I might kill!

Reaching the summit, we cheered our accomplishment with what breath we had left. One of the party made the observation, "Oh ****! Even the bears wouldn't come up here." As I was resting on a "soft" rock eating my lunch of a pilot biscuit mounded with reconstituted freeze-dried tuna salad, another of our party told me there were two eyes under my "soft" rock. One doesn't realize what reserve strength one has when "something" is five inches under one's butt. Would you believe it turned out to be two aluminum cans?

Amazing beauty surrounded us as we descended from the summit. Cold rushing streams, glorious evergreens, and blue, blue skies – we couldn't get enough of nature's gifts.

We enjoyed fresh trout for dinner as my husband somehow managed to catch enough to feed us all. Sleep comes easily with a full stomach and a cozy sleeping bag.

By the next day I was really ready for a hot shower. Instead, I nearly had a heart attack splashing in a frigid snow melt lake.

We were like horses sensing the barn as our fourth day arrived. The weather was deteriorating a bit so we marched downhill faster. Our destination was Agnew Meadows on the upper San Joaquin River drainage where we would catch a tour shuttle for our ride up the hill to the Mammoth Mountain ski area. We formed a circle and took a photo of our six pairs of boots (a real keepsake) as we waited for the shuttle.

I do have one regret. As we boarded the shuttle, all passengers stopped talking and stared at the six of us. Admittedly, we were dirty and tired with dusty backpacks that we stored inside the shuttle. This was in comparison to the relatively clean tourists already seated on the shuttle. We were exceedingly proud of what we had accomplished together. My regret – not announcing to the other passengers what we had seen, experienced, accomplished, and shared. We dearly loved being together for those thirty-six memorable miles.

Our kids still shake their heads!

RECOLLECTIONS OF THE GREATEST GENERATION

After the school bus dropped me off, I climbed the tall tower on snow covered stairs. It was wartime in the state of Washington. We lived at Puget Sound and were active in whatever we could do for the war effort. My mother volunteered to be an aircraft spotter. Around the clock it was a spotter's job to identify aircraft and call in by telephone to headquarters. Our call name was "Charlie 19". It was my job to carry the tea kettle from the hotplate back down the stairs (and there were what seemed like over a hundred stairs), fill the kettle with clean snow, and return to the top of the tower. The snow melted in the kettle and we had a nice cup of steaming tea. I treasure a photograph of my mother and I during those days. We were looking for enemy aircraft and I was pretending to be big stuff at age six.

We cultivated and shared the bounty from a community Victory Garden and used our wartime ration stamps to buy other staples.

Giant shadows grew larger and larger as the aircraft carrier sailed closer to me and Mike in our 12-foot row boat. I am seven years old; Mike is my Boston Terrier, ageless. We welcomed yet another war-torn ship home to Puget Sound. Weary sailors waved and, no doubt, wept at our feeble attempt of welcoming them home. Jagged holes just above the water line were to be repaired, preparing the carrier for yet another Pacific mission. Our welcoming activity over, Mike and I threw fishing lines under the floating logs close by, catching several sole for dinner that evening. Sixty-nine years later, I realize what unique joys I experienced, even in wartime. Mike, as always, would agree.

After some seventy years, I have visited Pacific Islands and viewed areas of Naval operations in both the Pacific and European theatres. I have stood on Omaha and Utah beaches and walked amid the 9000 graves in the American cemetery in France. And I have visited countries, cities, and towns in the European war zones where our troops were active. All of this leaves me with a sobering and deep admiration for those men and women who fought for our American way of life in WWII.

DOROTHY BACHELOR

Dorothy Bachelor was born in New York in 1930, relocated to Canoga Park, California, in the 1950s, and since 1973 has made the Antelope Valley her home. She and husband Carl now reside in Lancaster. In addition to being a true female pioneer as one of the first women to work on the assembly of the Space Shuttle, she somehow found the time to raise eight children. Dorothy is a talented storyteller who enjoys writing children's stories and amazing tales of her past experiences.

AN EVENT IN MY LIFE

I wore white cotton gloves and was dressed in Rockwell blues, the uniform of a TPS (Thermal Protection System) mechanic. I leaned out over a space three stories above a concrete floor, reached across approximately two feet and gently placed the silicone-based 4" x 4" black tile on the substrate of the vertical stabilizer. Previously, I had prepared the substrate by cleaning it with MEK and TRIKE, toxic industrial solvents, and had placed strips of reusable felt insulation along specified lines marked according to a Cartesian scale map.

It was a job I took pride in - the entire episode in my life that was my employment with Rockwell International. I was installing the thermal protection tiles on Columbia STS-1, the first Space Shuttle, which was launched from Cape Kennedy in Florida on April 12, 1981. From an historical viewpoint, I was part of a pioneer effort to breach the boundaries of space. I was also part of the general change in social attitudes affecting women - in particular, older women.

In order to get the job in the first place, I had to state unequivocally that I felt there was some discrimination involved. Discrimination had become the bug-a-boo word of the 1970s, and it was a sure-fire attention getter. The employment officer tried to discourage me by intimidating me with statements to the effect that I had no experience whatsoever in the line of installing thermal protection tiles. I rebutted this instantly with statements to the effect that neither had anyone else. This was something that had never been done before, so how could anyone have any experience at it?

The job called for delicacy of handling an object and the ability to follow instructions. I qualified. I had diapered many babies without sticking pins in either myself or the baby, and I had successfully created gourmet meals from recipes. As for dealing with toxic chemicals, any housecleaning chore demanded that particular skill, and I certainly didn't need a degree in chemistry to tell me not to mix Clorox with Comet. I could also read blueprints, having put together bicycles on Christmas Eve and constructed toys that were supposed to be so simple a child could put them together, yet they defied a great many adults.

Whichever argument persuaded the employment officials, I was hired and became a part of the history of this country. I did believe in all that I had said, that I could handle almost anything. I had raised eight children, was healthy, and the world was my oyster. I didn't even consider that being 51 years old had anything to do with my capability to function effectively in this instance. I do not consider that chronological age has any bearing on most circumstances.

So that is how I became part of Rockwell's token-type employee group, fulfilling mandated quotas for affirmative action. I was the only female in a class of about fifteen males. The instructor made that an obvious fact. However, I passed the final exam, second highest and third finished. To that extent, I felt I had participated in the changing social scene, the changing attitudes toward women, a giant step forward along the new frontier, and so forth.

The whole thing was not without its humorous moments. At one point, we were being instructed on the different types of Frisi, the insulative felt applied to the shuttle. We were crouched down under the opened cargo bay doors, and I forgot about the inflexibility of them as I stood up to ease my aching muscles and "whanged" my head on the overhead door. "Whanged" is the only word to describe it because the whole group could hear the resounding WHANNNNG as my skull hit the titanium wall of the cargo bay door.

The instructor looked over with concern, inquiring how I felt and was I alright and that sort of thing. At that point several things happened. Fireworks went off in my head and my sight was flecked with shooting sparks, but my instinct was to be blasé, to be laid back, cool. I just rubbed my skull a little, shrugged it off, and assured them it was nothing; I was perfectly okay, not to fuss. There was no way in the world I was going to admit to even a twinge of pain. I was not going to interrupt this instructive tour, and I was not going to become an object of concern on my first day on the job. It earned me the sobriquet of "hard-head." And I was.

I suffered aches and pains in places that I didn't even know were a part of my body, but I put tiles on that shuttle. The first Columbia mission flew thirty-six earth orbits and landed at Edwards AFB, California, on April 14, 1981. As later was to be seen, my tiles were not one of those that was stripped off during re-entry. In more ways than one, I was part of history in the making.

PAT ALEXANDER

Born and raised in Buffalo, New York, and having lived in several U.S. states and in Europe, Pat Alexander is happy to call the Antelope Valley's high desert her home.

Pat is multi-talented; she is an artist as well as a published author, and also worked in the entertainment industry. While living abroad she studied art in Milan, Paris, and Dubrovnik, and has exhibited and sold her paintings worldwide. She was also a principal entertainer, singing and dancing for eight years with the Folies Bergère and other stage shows in Las Vegas.

She discovered her writing talent in California, where she began composing short stories and poetry. Pat published her first book, *Pollywogs and Green Things Growing*, in 2011. She is currently working on two more projects: a sequel to her first book which will include her artwork, and a memoir of her years as a Vegas entertainer. She hopes to have both published in 2015.

GOD'S FACE

I see Gods' face imprinted in the stars

I view His countenance

Stretched across heavenly horizons

In the glory of all earth's sunrises and sunsets

I am God's eyes, beholding God.

BABY OTTO

The Folies Bergere was a variety show. We had many acts that made up the program. Some of the most unpredictable were the animal acts. We had a magician named "The Fabulous George Monroe." In his act he used six white doves, two white rabbits named Dotty and Ditto, and a Burmese boa constrictor named Charlie. He was very accomplished at his craft and the audience appreciated it.

The night that Charlie went missing was serious. George needed him for the finale. First the magician would show the audience two rabbits, Dotty and Ditto. He would put his cloak over them causing them to disappear into thin air. Later, he pulled Dotty from his top hat. But when he put his hand in the hat the second time, he slowly withdrew the long, spotted snake, Charlie. The audience figured poor Ditto must have been devoured by Charlie. This always got a good reception with gasps of, "Oh no," from everyone. Well, tonight there was no Charlie! How could they have a finale without him?

Everyone in the show was put to the task of finding Charlie. Five minutes before the curtain was about to go up, a heart-stopping scream was heard from the showgirls' dressing room. Felicia was yelling, "Help, there is a snake in my hat! Anyone, please come and save me." Poor Felicia had a terrible fear of snakes. She had been raised in the Outback in Australia and wanted nothing to do with snakes, wild or tame. We all came running to behold Charlie curled up and fast asleep in Felicia's large, feathered headdress.

George Monroe was a bit strange, as I imagine some magicians can be. His favorite pet, Cookie, was a praying mantis that he wore on his shoulder, connected by a tiny, thin golden chain. The insect was a bright green color and was at least five or six inches long. He sat perched on George's black satin lapel of his tuxedo, usually cleaning and preening his mandibles in expectation of another yummy meal to come. Some of the chorus girls would bring Cookie tasty live bugs just to see him devour them. Cookie was grateful for these treats and never turned any away. After first eating its head, he would hold the body in his claws and munch on it as a person would an ear of corn. There were never any 'leftovers'. Cookie was good-natured and would allow you to stroke him. He feared neither man nor beast. He was a premier predator. George said that he was the most fascinating critter he had ever seen and we unanimously agreed, "He sure is, George, he sure is," as we watched Cookie polishing off a big, fat, brown grasshopper!

One night, during the dinner show, we were to go on stage following Fred Wilson's Fantastic Chimpanzees. This act consisted of four chimps: Darla, the mom; Destin, the pop; Junior, the son; and Baby Otto. Fred Wilson, the animal trainer, always dressed them in adorable costumes that they hated to wear. This particular night, Baby Otto tore off all of his clothes and his diaper and was throwing handfuls of poop at the audience. "Stop him, stop him," Al, the stage manager, was exhorting Fred Wilson who was desperately trying to catch Baby Otto. By now, the chimp had leaped into the orchestra pit and was wrestling a trombone from a musician. The poor guy cried, "Ouch! Get him off me!" as Baby Otto bit him on his hand for not handing over the instrument. "Grab him for me, guys, will you?" cried Fred, as he dove into the pit trying to reach his run-a-way chimp. Pandemonium broke loose as the musicians tried to escape the little monster.

Baby Otto screamed, "whoo, whoo, whoo, eek, eek, eek," at all of them. He was having the greatest fun being free and out of control. "Eek, eek, eek, uka, uka," Baby Otto squealed as he pursed his lips and spat at his keeper just as Fred Wilson grabbed hold of him, put a leash over his neck, and hauled him off the stage. Bob, the bitten musician, got an antibiotic injection from the hotel doctor. He was shaken up but bravely returned to the orchestra to finish his set with the band.

"Hey Bob, it's all part of the job. The show must go on, right?" agreed the musicians. Poor Bob still looked frazzled but reached for his trombone and blew a few notes to get back in the groove with the guys.

FULL MOON

In the darkness of the night
    Our lovely Sister Moon appears.
Lighting up the sky and bestowing her love-glow
    Upon us, her family.

She reaches out to us from on high
    Soothing our minds and hearts
Proving once more just how much
    She cares for us.

We are filled with her moon shine
    Our bodies accept the light and love as
We are rendered happy and content.
Forgetting our cares, becoming closer to one another
    We accomplish something extraordinary.

A oneness permeates our being with all creation.
    A promise to make everything right in our universe
Even though our souls are adrift on our tiny, blue water planet.
    Our Sister Moon comforts us and makes us believe in love
Every even-tide as she once again shows her beautiful face to us,
    Her adoring family.

WINTER IN ANTELOPE VALLEY

The rainbow mountains of Tehachapi are snowbound
In the stillness of a winter's day.
Massive peaks illuminated in the sunset's glow
Astride their wide, white shoulders.
They shrug off the frigid air and turn toward
Father Sun who smiles upon them as he sends
Flocks of ravens and blackbirds to nest in the
Green fir trees, alive on their flanks.

A small herd of Mule deer daintily pick their way,
Making paths in the drifts, pawing through the snow
To uncover just enough food for one more day.

A tawny mountain lion and her half-grown cub are
Living in a cave overlooking the valley.
She has caught two large jackrabbits to share,
To fill their bellies against the cold, bringing deep
Slumber as they curl around one another for warmth.

The mountain God looks on with love for the animals,
Always providing for them.

LANCASTER BOULEVARD

The city of Lancaster has a wonderful new boulevard. It is the heart of the city. Everything here is brand new or remodeled. There are many kinds of young green trees, the most prevalent being Sycamores, Elms, and Mimosas. In the center strip you can park your car under the trees. Both sides of The Boulevard for many blocks are lined with fabulous shops and restaurants. Some have outdoor patios in front where you can sit and hobnob with other folks eating and drinking, watching the people and the cars glide slowly by. It is a true promenade.

While strolling, you can meet and greet old friends and make new ones, too. On one corner bands are frequently playing on the podium built especially for this reason. There is a movie theatre with reclining seats that serves food and drinks while you watch first-run films.

MOAH, the new three-story art gallery and museum is open for your pleasure. Across the street and up a block is the Performing Arts Center with classical performances like ballet and big-name entertainers. There is literally something for everyone to experience.

On Thursdays there is a farmers' market and many kiosks and tents are set up to serve foods such as chicken or beef on a stick, ice cream, hummus, hot dogs, and honey. There are tacos and tostados, chimichangas and fried dough waffles with sugar and whipped cream. All delicious to eat. Also many vegetable stands line the street, some with exotic oriental goodies like lemon grass and big daikon radishes; lots of cherries, peaches, plums and apples; and home-made jars of pickled sauerkraut. There are baked goods such as apple and berry pie or strudel. Some stands have ladies knock-off handbags and lovely scarves or hand-knitted baby clothes, booties, and caps. What a good time you will have just sauntering along sampling foods or gazing at some pretty pieces of jewelry.

Tables and chairs with umbrellas are set up in front of the bandstand at Bex restaurant so you can sit and eat your Poor Boy sandwich while listening to a great Rock or Western band. Sometimes in the adjoining courtyard they have ribs and chicken with corn on the cob for only five dollars. So tasty!

On occasion we go to see our friends who own the Pueblo Viejo restaurant. "Hi Josephine." We greet one another warmly. They serve great food like papusas, beef stew, and chicken with rice. Order a large bottle of El Salvadorian beer to go along with the food and you will be *contenta*, for sure.

On Halloween night The Boulevard comes alive with ghosts and Batmen, Supermen, Spidermen, witches, Frankensteins, Ozzie Osbournes, and all sorts of creatures walking up and down the street showing off their costumes. Dress up and you may win a prize for the most innovative costume. This year they even had a troop doing a dance from a Broadway play.

Halloween is the biggest turnout on The Boulevard next to the Christmas celebration, with a parade to boot. Then there is a weekend in September where go-carts race up and down the street for prizes, and another weekend that features America the Beautiful and our veterans. One attraction displays antique cars parked up and down The Boulevard.

I say, "Come one, come all," but do come to the Lancaster Boulevard and promenade. You will love the experience!

CREATION

From the dust of stars, an orange-red globe rages
into fiery life------ glowing hot.
Pulsing, growing, expanding, ever outward.
Shooting out, into the void of space.
Eons later, the planet Earth, revolving, spins fast, faster,
Then slow, slower yet, turning on its axis as
it accepts, cradles, and nourishes alien beings
alighting on its yet warm body.
Gases of creation, the myriad forms evolve,
they boom, ripen, mature, only to slip away,
again, and again, into oblivion.
Other lives become, rise out from the
Primordial oozes------creeping, crawling, slithering,
they divide themselves a thousand-fold,
spit out progeny-------- to begin anew.
Infinitesimal seedlings take root, pushing up green fronds
in Earth's rich, virgin soil.
Other strange forms of life develop, some wearing fins and scales.
The age of the Dinosaurs has arrived.

ESPERANZA BELTRAN

Esperanza Beltran is a wife and stay-at-home mom, tutor, cook, story-reader, nurse, taxi driver and more to three beautiful children. When she was growing up, she enjoyed writing poems and songs, drawing and painting. But as she grew older, and her family grew larger, she mostly put aside her artistic endeavors, deciding that they had only been childhood dreams. Occasionally she wrote in her journal and doodled on sheets of paper but never took any of it seriously. Recently, things changed when she decided to begin recording a very important moment in her life. The journal she had started led to the story she has always wanted to tell - the amazing life of her paternal grandmother who grew up in Mexico. She now spends her days trying to find time to paint and to write the book about her grandmother's struggles and accomplishments.

SLIDING INTO FEAR

This story is about the day I drowned in compete silence. Nauj had been pestering me about getting up on the water slide and sliding into the pool. "What's the big deal?" he had asked, completely astonished that I had no desire to get on. I mean, why would I not want to slide into three feet of water? Simple, I was terrified!

You see, I don't know how to swim. I will get into a pool but as soon as the water level raises to anywhere close to my face I freak out. I will definitely and absolutely never dunk my head underwater, and playing in the pool makes my heart beat at a million per second. If trying to enjoy a fun game of aquatic basketball, the possibility of tripping and falling face first into the water is the only thought my mind can conceive. Needless to say, I don't enjoy myself much inside a pool, and my son's insistence on my sliding into possible death was completely absurd.

"Look," he said as he marched himself up the ladder to the top of the slide, "you just sit and then let go."

It seemed easy enough to go up the ladder and sit on the slide, it was the letting go part that seemed just a little too hard to do. Nauj smiled as he went down the slide and very smoothly landed on his two feet, his face never touching the water which was just an inch above his waist. He did this not once or twice but uncountable times, not only to show me this was possible to do even when one does not know how to swim, but for the most part because he was having fun.

Nauj is ten years old; he is more on the lighter side and is close to reaching the five foot mark. At five and six years old I had him in swim lessons in which he reached level two. Level two consists of knowing how to put one's head underwater and knowing some basic strokes that will allow one to move in the water without having to touch the bottom of the pool. In short, he learned how to doggy paddle. Yes, that is as far as he got, and yet he has no problem with going down a water slide or canon-balling himself into four feet of water. How that is possible, I have no idea. It could be because he is a Capricorn and I'm not one hundred percent sure but Capricorns have something to do with nature and water. I'm sure that's it; that's the reason he can accomplish these crazy feats. Me, I'm a Taurus and as such I prefer having my feet on solid ground.

"Come on, Ma," he insisted again after a while of having left me alone.

"Yeah," added my daughter, the high school team swimmer.

"No." I laughed an I-want-to-but-I-can't kind of laugh. But they were starting to convince me. I don't yet know what it was that pushed me to finally say yes to my kids and accept the possibility of an early death. I know it wasn't because of their pestering. I've grown accustomed enough to it that I don't often give in. It could've been the fact that my aquatic little son made it seem so easy. I mean, he landed on his two feet, so how bad could it be? Chances are I would land on my own two feet as well; after all, we are almost similar in height. Or maybe it was just that I was tired of being scared.

In an instant I got up from the steps of the pool where I had been so comfortably sitting with my kin, my three year old son, Gael, and started making my way to the slide's ladder. Just as I had predicted, moving up the ladder was very easy. I went up each step without thinking much about the future that awaited me. Sitting on the top of the slide was also pretty easy, I've sat on top of slides many times in my life and had no problem doing so one more time. So I sat,…and I sat,… and I sat. Sitting there, I noticed I had a pretty amazing view from my position.

The sky was big and clear and blue, just like the ocean that reflected it across the horizon. The dry desert landscape never looked so welcoming with the muted tones of its prickly sand and ocotillo plants, cacti and creosote bushes. I imagined that maybe I could just sit there and take in the view for while. Why not? I wasn't in a hurry after all. But the 'come on's' and 'just go's' coming from my kids at the bottom of the slide awakened me from my trance.

Everyone was so focused on me that they had forgotten about my little one. "Check on Gael," I yelled, looking around for him. Gael was just fine and happily playing with the dirt in the potted plants that lined the side of the pool where the slide and I stiffly sat. He had no idea that he was about to lose his mother. Poor thing. Thank goodness Gael and the potted plants were far enough away that there was no danger that he'd fall into the pool, but still I tried to get everyone to focus on him. *Don't worry about me, I'll be fine,* I imagined myself saying. My husband, who had been resting outside of the pool and quietly watching this whole situation unravel, reminded me that, from his position, he had a perfect view of both Gael and me. With the iPhone in his hands he eagerly awaited the moment that I would eventually slide down.

"Maaa!" yelled Mayerlin and Nauj, "Come on, just let go!"

They were starting to get annoyed with me, I think. Mayerlin, the swimmer, promised to stay there. At 5' 2.5" and one-hundred forty pounds of mostly muscle she seemed to tower over my 5' and one-hundred pound petite self. I had no doubt that she could pull me out of the water if she needed to.

My mind started creating some nonsensical pictures. I imagined Mayerlin standing at the bottom of the slide, legs spread out, knees bent, and leaning forward with extended arms saying, "Come on," with a huge smile. The way I had done for her years ago. But no, I thought, I'm not two years old and my one-hundred pounds going at 100 mph could hurt her. Maybe she could just extend her arm to stop me from going too far into the pool, I thought, but still that seemed like she would get hurt. How in the world was she going to keep my face from plunging into the water? Oh, wait, I was going to land on my feet! But what if I didn't? Well, Nauj did it and he's only ten so I should be able to do it. Wait, where's Gael? Okay, there he is. My kids are too close to the slide; I could hurt them. Maybe I should just turn around and get off of the slide. No, that's dangerous, too. This damn slide is too slippery and so much higher than it looks from below. Maybe if it was just a little lower I could've slid down by now. Ugh, who am I kidding? Why the heck am I so scared?!!!

"OK," I said, "I'm going."

I lifted my right hand to my nose, pinched it hard, held on tight to the slide with my left, and then slowly started letting my butt move just an inch down the slide. I saw everyone's face light up with excitement and . . . I stopped.

"Ahhh, Maaa!" I heard my kids complain from below. I laughed. I had fooled them. No, I had fooled myself. I really was planning on letting go, but then my fear got the best of me and I just couldn't.

One more time I sat there thinking about a million reasons why I should not do this. I could drown, that's a big one. But in reality I knew I wouldn't because my daughter or my husband, I would like to think, would jump in to save me. Then, there were a lot of other little reasons. Water will get into my ears and that's very uncomfortable. Water could get into my nose and that's also very uncomfortable, and it was not something I wanted to deal with. Unfortunately, my logical side chimed in and let me know that neither of these was such a big deal; they'd pass.

Then my dad came into the picture and took over my thoughts. Just that morning I had talked to him over the phone. I had lied to him telling him we were in San Francisco when in reality we were in the complete opposite direction, San Felipe. I had lied, not wanting to make an excuse as to why we should not drive down south to the rehab center, where he had agreed to go a week earlier.

"We'll be there tomorrow," I had said, without giving any specifics, but I knew he knew. I knew he was scared, terrified just like I was sitting on top of this water slide. He was scared of finding out what was beyond the alcohol, the pain he would have to deal with if he no longer had a beer to cushion it. He was afraid of letting go of the only life he knew. I was afraid of not being able to hide behind my fear anymore, of letting go and sinking into the unknown with really no logical reason for my fear.

I thought of all the times I had been frustrated with him for being afraid, for not being able to drop the beer and start anew. Couldn't he see how amazing life was; how good his life could be if he just stepped out of the darkness that his fear held him in? Couldn't he see that his fears were completely illogical? That everything would be just fine?

Damn it! I was right. There was no logical reason for me to be afraid; all is okay down there. Just like my brother and I would be there for my dad, my kids were down there just for me. They would not let me drown. Right? Right!

I let go . . .

I closed my eyes and held on tight to my nose all the way down the slide which seemed to go on forever. It wasn't at 100 mph as I had predicted; it was more like 101 mph and it was the scariest feeling I could ever have imagined. My chest was hot from the terrible, crazy beating of my heart which seemed to be stuck in my throat.

The water splashed as it opened up to receive me and cover me whole. I didn't land on my feet as I had predicted. I landed clumsily, in a fetal position.

In the water, I had to let go of my nose and start flapping away to save myself because my kids didn't seem to be doing anything to get me out of there. Wasn't my daughter going to pull me out? She wasn't supposed to let me sink all the way in! It was so quiet down there; I couldn't hear a thing. And except for the drama that I was creating underwater, all was peaceful.

After an hour of being down there, or what felt like an hour, and having to save myself because nobody came to my rescue, I set my feet to the bottom of the pool, lifted my head and triumphantly stood up in the three-foot high water. "HA! I win!" I smiled and we all laughed.

The feeling of conquering my fear was far stronger than the suffocating feeling of being afraid. I felt like I could take on the world if I wanted to, so I went up the slide again. This time no coercing was needed.

Again fear took the best of me and again I sat there. This time, however, I did not sit there for twenty minutes like I had last time. This time it was only five minutes. I held on tight to my nose and again…I let go.

The silence of being under water, I think, is what called me to slide down again. I was in love. Everyone was happy and I was elated.

"Can you put your head underwater now?" Mayerlin asked with a huge hopeful smile.

"I don't know," I said, "Let me see."

I pinched my nose and without giving it a second thought I submerged myself into the water as my kids stood around to watch me. Although it didn't last long, because I can only hold my breath for about two seconds, underneath that water I felt a certain kind of peace I had never felt before. I popped back up and smiled.

"You see," my daughter announced, "You just had to get over a little fear to get over a big one."

Fears, big or small, can hold back so much of you, it's surprising. We smiled and got out of the pool, leaving it in the quiet, undisturbed state we had found it in, as if nothing had happened. I walked away having started a new relationship, one that looked very promising.

JACKIE L. CROSSWHITE SR.

Jackie started writing songs when he was only twelve years old. He was born and raised in Mississippi, and his love of Rock and Roll and Country-western music stems from his Southern roots. He owns the filed copyrights to his many lyrics, some which have been set to music and recorded.

At age 22 he moved to Southern California and resided in a number of cities before settling his family in the Antelope Valley. A Ford Motor Company retiree, he now resides in Lancaster and loves the perfect weather and open space of desert living. He enjoys being an active member of the AVWA, and this is his second time writing for their anthologies. Jackie manages to instill his quaint Mississippi country flavor into his writing. He is currently working on three books: his memoirs, fictional short stories, and a novel.

COO-COO BIRD
The bird flew over
he never came back again
Coo-Coo clock ate him

STARING
Look once and look twice
but do not look a third time
That is called staring

AROUND THE WORLD
You go to the North
I will go to the South
We may meet someplace

MY GUARDIAN ANGELS

My Guardian Angels watched over me and protected me during my stay in the hospital when I had my heart surgery. Some say that there are no such things as Angels. I know that they are out there because I have seen them.

On February 4, 2009, I had two major heart attacks within a two-hour time frame. I was thinking indigestion and ulcers in my stomach, because I had been treated for problems like that. So I went to the urgent care clinic instead of going to the emergency room at the hospital. After blood tests and electrocardiograms the doctors said that I was having major heart attacks, and I needed emergency surgery. So they rushed me to the Antelope Valley Hospital.

At the emergency intensive care unit, the doctors found out that I needed four-bypass heart surgery, the granddaddy of them all, and I needed it right away. But I had already been given blood thinners, so they could not do surgery for several days. So, meanwhile, they kept me in intensive care until my surgery time on February 11.

During my stay in intensive care, I was seeing Angels.

Not just one, but eight Angels, maybe more. I was seeing them all at the same time, and not just once in a while, but most of the time while I was awake. I was on the fourth floor of the hospital, so it was not like I was on the ground floor and maybe seeing people outside the window.

Outside of my big picture window was a small ledge about two feet wide, probably used by maintenance personnel while working on the building or cleaning windows. I could see two people on the ledge outside the window looking in at me. On the right-hand side of the window I could see this head only peeking in and looking at me. It always had a hood on, so I could not tell if it was a man or a woman. On the left-hand side of the window I could see a man in a suit looking at me. I could also see the building across the way. On the ledge and the roof of that building I could see eight people looking toward my window. I could not tell if they were men or women as they moved around up there. These people looked so real that at first I figured that maybe our President was here for some reason, and these were his security agents.

In my room, I could see through the wall into the room next to me and I could see people in there moving around. I would always focus in on the same lady every time. She was talking to people in there. I could not hear what she was saying, but I thought that she was the Virgin Mary.

Also, there were three pictures hanging on the wall in my room. I could stare at them and they would change to different pictures. Sometimes they would change to writings that I could not read. I figured that all of the illusions that I was having were caused by the medicines that the doctors were giving me. I kept seeing the same people and things over and over. None of the images that I saw ever talked to me. I think if I was hallucinating that I would see different images each time, not the same things repeatedly. And what I was seeing would not have had anything to do with the President, even if he was there. So that made me believe that I was seeing my Guardian Angels.

A friend of mine who is very religious came to visit me the day before my surgery, and I told him about this and asked him if it was possible that I could be seeing Angels? He said that yes it could be and most likely was, because God has his Angels all around hospitals and places where people are sick, to care and to protect them.

I went through my surgery and recovery without any problems, and on February 17, after spending fourteen days in intensive care, I went home.

For those who are non-believers, I believe that God has his Angels all over the world helping him to watch over his people. And I know that I saw something that I could not really explain. It could have been the medicine causing illusions, but until I am proven wrong, I'll stick to my story that my Guardian Angels protected me.

I AM A WINNER

When I was a kid in 1949, I was a marble-toting, straight-shooting son of a cowboy in Canton, Mississippi. I was a twelve-year old boy in a family of nine siblings. So you can understand what it was like for us kids as far as toys were concerned. Toys were at the bottom of the want list of things to buy each week. That meant that you didn't get what you wanted unless you made it or went out and worked to buy it.

The game of marbles is a very simple game and it costs very little to own. I could buy a bag of two-hundred marbles for ten cents, and share them with my three brothers, James, Alton, and Amail Jr. The only equipment necessary to play the game is a tree twig and a piece of chalk – the tree twig for drawing a five-foot bull ring in the dirt, and the chalk for drawing it on the concrete or blacktop. As far as the game rules go, every player antes up an equal amount of marbles into the center of the bull ring. The players have to lag to a line in order to set up the order of rotation to shoot. The lag line is a straight line touching the ring, and lagging is shooting a marble to be closest to the lag line.

The first player starts the game by shooting from the outside circle of the ring, shooting at the marbles in the ring and trying to knock them out of the ring. Each player must knock a marble out of the ring or give up his turn to the next player and go back to the end of the line. Players keep the marbles that they knock out of the ring. When the last marble is knocked out of the ring, the game is over. Then everyone antes up again for a new game.

I always had my pockets full of marbles, and my toy shooters in my hands. I was loaded for bear and ready to rumble, looking for some action from anyone game enough to take me on, and to lose their marbles. I was the top marble shooting "dog" in my neighborhood for beating up on anyone who wanted to take me on.

I went to the local Boys Club and entered the national marble shooting contest. It was a five level contest: city, county, state, national semi-finals, and national finals. At the first contest, the city championship, all of my friends showed up and played. I went through this tournament with a breeze. Won my first trophy ever and boy was she a beauty. The man in charge was my friend Dave.

He said that he would be my coach and from then on all expenses would be covered.

On the following Saturday we went to the county tournament in Jackson, Mississippi. It was a little tougher than the city meet because more players were involved. I won this tournament also. Boy! Two of these babies; how grateful I am.

The next Saturday was the state tournament. Dave said that this one covered more territory and that meant I had to be more careful. Make every move count. Well I soared through that tournament as if I knew what I was doing. I couldn't believe that I won the state title. The national semi-final and the national final were to be played in Washington D.C. in two weeks.

The night before the semis I had a dream that I was soaring way up in the sky with big birds, when all of a sudden a huge eagle with angel wings appeared beside me and said, "I'm Gary. Dave and I are your friends and we know that you can do this, Jack. Just believe in what you are doing and do the best that you can." Then the eagle disappeared as quickly as he had appeared. It seemed so real. I told Dave about it, and he said that it could be a good omen telling me that I will win the finals.

I won the semis, and the next day would be the finals. Boy, was I excited! My opponent's name was also Jack, and he was from Lancaster, California. Well I won the match and was the new United States Marble Shooting Champion. I made history in my home town. Dave said to me, "It's so amazing what you can do if you believe that you can do it."

Dave and his friend Gary became writers and they published a book about the tournament. They named it, "I AM A WINNER."

SEARCHING FOR ANYTHING

I keep asking myself, are all writers crazy, or do only crazy people write? Either way, by the time you finish reading this story you will have me tagged as crazy, not insane, but crazy as a koo-koo loony bird.

Now I have this assignment where I'm supposed to write a story about anything. I can't write about anything because I just don't know anything about anything anymore, so therefore, I will try and do the best that I can.

Once upon a time, not yesterday, not today, but sometime ago, I had Anything and everything. My wife, Anything, said that she was going to clean our house, not just dust it, but clean it from top to bottom, wall to wall. And she did. She cleaned it out okay, not the kind of cleaning that you do with soap and water, but the kind that you do with a truck and dolly.

After Anything took everything, not just some things in particular, but everything that we owned, she disappeared. Not appeared, but disappeared into the night, not in the day, but in the middle of the night to someplace unknown. Not this place, not that place, but someplace in between this and that and here and there, probably no place in particular, just anyplace where she can hide from me.

I was told by a friend that he saw Anything with Somebody, not anybody in particular, just Somebody that she knew. Ever since this happened, I have been searching everywhere for Anything, not just anywhere in particular, but everywhere where Anything and Somebody could be hiding.

Someday I will find Anything, maybe not today, maybe not tomorrow, no day in particular, but someday I will find her. I don't know what I will say to Anything when I see her again. I probably will say to her, "Honey come home, I need you, and I love you."

Until then, I'll keep searching for Anything. You probably think that I am crazy, and you're right, not wrong, but right. I'm as crazy as they come.

OFFEND
Did I offend you?
If I did then that's okay
I meant to do that

ONCE
You can do it once
and if that is not enough
do it once again

SHARE
Share and share alike
I have nothing in my hands
Share with me, okay

LOOKOUT
Look before you leap
has been said time after time
Ignore it and pay!

LIVE IT UP
Live to fulfillment
Forever is forever
Life is very short

MIA LEE

Mia Lee was born and raised in Korea. She left at age 22 to come to the United States and have a better life for her family. She has lived in California for the past 44 years, and now resides in Lancaster. She has taken on the huge task of writing her life story, which includes the hardships she endured as a child caught up in the Korean War, and the highs and lows of being an immigrant in America. The following story is an excerpt from her memoirs.

MY THANKSGIVING DAY

Early January 1977, my world crumbled and went dark. All the oxygen sucked out of my body. I couldn't breathe. It's as if I was in a dream and falling into a bottomless pit. This is the end of my life, I thought. All I could hear was my own voice calling out to my children.

How could any human be so evil and so cruel as to take away children from their mother? The damages caused to my children are unforgivable. I could not imagine what they were going through. Suddenly one day they have no mother and no home.

I went to school to pick them up after work, but no sign of them. I went to see the principal, and she told me my kids didn't come to school that day. I thought, they must have gone to the zoo, or a museum, but as night approached I started to worry more. I began calling their friends. No one had seen them. I called places where Don, my ex-husband, worked; they hadn't seen or heard from him or the kids either. Now I am panicking, wondering what might have happened to them. I called the police and made a report, but they didn't seem too concerned. I called their grandmother – nothing.

Now I was pacing the house staring at the phone to ring. It was getting late. I had to do something. I started driving around the streets where they might have gone, hoping to find them. Nothing! I cried all night, and then the next morning I started driving the streets again. I went to the police station. It did not seem we were important enough; no one seemed to care.

Many days and nights I was still hoping, staring at the door and phone. They could still walk through the door or call me. Days went by; weeks went by, now months had gone. I had a sick feeling; they were really gone. I guessed that my life was over. Without my children I had nothing. They were my life. But I kept searching. I called airlines, bus stations, train stations, hospitals, junkyards, anybody and anyplace I could think of. No hope. No help.

I hired private investigators, but they could not find anything either. They said that someone had wiped clean all of their government documents. They had all disappeared like they never existed. Someone told me I needed a lawyer, so that is what I did next. The lawyer was very sympathetic and very kind. She thought I should go see a psychiatrist since I was in a very bad condition mentally and physically.

I needed help. The last few months I hadn't eaten or slept much. I had lost 20% of my weight. My brain was so exhausted that it did not function anymore. But everyone told me that I must go on, and one day I will find my children. I had no choice but to believe them and keep living until that day. Not knowing whether my kids were alive or dead, my heart was torn into a million pieces. I kept praying that they were safe and happy somewhere. Maybe they will think about me once and a while and miss me. I tried to be a good mother and a good person. Now I wondered if only I could have done things differently, maybe I would still have my children. It must be all my fault. I would do anything - give up my soul, my body - anything to have my kids back by my side.

Throughout the next fifteen years I tried every lead. Now I was just surviving, but still hoping that maybe someday I would wake up from this nightmare and feel the sun on my face and smile again with my kids by my side. So many support group meetings; so many people going through the same nightmare as I am. I found out there are thousands of them every year. I would not have believed that such a thing could happen, if it didn't happen to me. I never thought that people could be so mean.

I never moved or changed phone numbers. Someday they will have to come; someday they will be old enough to be on their own and they will come home.

I have a very dear friend who became my family since he was an orphan. He was always supportive no matter what I did. One day he sent me a book about people with the same last name as me and my children. I put the book away without looking at it, thinking to myself that it was of no use, and I forgot about it.

It was 1992, and I was in Hawaii when I broke up with my boyfriend. I went back to my home, but could not live with my brother and his family who were staying at my house. My brother had been living with me since 1977, and then he got married and had two kids. From day one, my sister-in-law and me never got along. But I wanted to help my brother so I let them stay in my house. My sister-in-law came to the U.S.A. with one suitcase and moved into my house and I let her have everything in it. I cannot describe the terrible things she did and how she treated my brother. She just used him to come to America. Once she got here she didn't care about anyone or anything but herself. This is why I decided to go away from my home. In 1995, my mother decided to come to the States and thank goodness my sister-in-law did not want to live with my mother. So I told them to move out and I went back to my home where my children were born.

I was thinking about my daughter one day and decided to visit the hospital where she was born. It brought back many happy memories. That night I couldn't sleep so I watched television at 2:30 in the morning. A show was on about people who found each other after thirty years of no contact. My eyes opened wide and I began to shake. My heart raced with hope. I searched for and found the book my friend had sent me long ago and began looking for names. First I saw my ex's name, but he has a common name so I tried not to get excited. I continued to look for my son's and my daughter's names. My daughter has a very unusual name, and when I saw it in the book I could not believe it. This must be a trick; I am seeing things, I told myself. I took a deep breath and looked again. Her name was still in the book. I started writing down all of the information that she will need to confirm that I am her mother. I couldn't wait until the Post Office opened. I sent the information in overnight mail.

Every second seemed forever, hours gone by, days gone by. My hope began to diminish. I guessed it was another dead end, like so many times before. I wasn't as lucky as some of these people on T.V. My life will just have to go on.

But one afternoon a couple of weeks later, I was taking a shower and my phone rang. Without even turning off the water, I answered it. He was looking for his mother, he said. "My name is Jae."

I told him it was not very nice to pull such a cruel joke on people. He said he really was looking for his mother. He got the letter that I had sent. At that moment I dropped the phone and sank into the bathtub, the water still running down on me. I paid no attention and just started sobbing. I am sure my son did not understand what I was saying because I tried to talk while I was crying. He explained how he got the mail from his sister. "All I want to do is see them," I told him. I will come to him right now and we can go to Lia.

I must have sounded like a crazy woman. I calmed myself down and thought about how we can do this, and a light bulb came on. It was less than a couple of weeks from Thanksgiving. "Why don't we all meet at my house for Thanksgiving?" I told him.

It seemed like forever, waiting for the day to come. "I have waited this long, I can wait a few more days," I told myself. I asked my son to send me some pictures so I would recognize him. Finally, the day came and we all went to the airport, LAX. I saw him right away. We held each other and cried; I never wanted to let him go. Lia drove all the way from New Jersey. She met us at the house. We all stood on the sidewalk hugging and crying.

What a day! I had my life back. I could finally breathe again and enjoy my children again. What a blessing! What a joy on this holiday of giving thanks. It was MY Thanksgiving Day, to remember forever.

GINA HUDGENS

Gina Hudgens hails from the Republic of the Philippines, in an old town that dates back to the Spanish era. She earned her B.S. degree in Accounting and Business at La Salle University (ICC-La Salle), and a B.S. in Education in Manila. She also studied Computer Programming.

Her overflowing joy and love for life and family is her greatest inspiration in writing. Her childhood memories growing up in the islands has shaped her into the fun-loving person that she is today. She thankfully dedicates this journey that she is embarking on, the art of writing, to her dear and sweet, loving family: Greg, Vanessa, and Stella.

INSPIRED

Open Doors and Open Windows,
Opportunity knocks and Discovery.

Youthful Beauty and Wholesome Health,
Confidence Bloom and Faith Endures.

Nutritious Food and Delicious Drinks,
Bring you Peace and Simply Joy.

Slumber Sleep and Sweet Dreams,
Love and Aspiration.

WILL YOU

Throw a kiss
To the night
Bright yellow moon.

Whisper your wishes
But be sincere and pure
Then cross your heart.

Knock your knees
And stomp your feet
Toe raises, up down.

Turn around, chin up
Make a slight bow
And politely say,

Moon,
Please grant my wishes,
Will You?

A GIRLS' NIGHT OUT

Gertrude is a dear close and long lost friend of mine.
Tonight is our Girls' Night Out and all is going fine.
Anticipation built high to make this a special event.
Forgetting the fact, she just arrived from a long flight.

No need to worry for she is like a pro,
She wants to go out as much as I do.
With the wave of a wand all is under control,
We glammed up together, like a fashion patrol.

Sparkle and glitter with red chameleon gloss,
Blush-n-brighten with wild sultry rouge.
Her four-inch red Prada shoes and my Vera Wang coat,
Looking chic, but I don't care much for her cashmere goat.

A quick glance of her diamond ring the size of a dime,
Engaged, and to celebrate it not would be a crime.
Her cougar years are numbered and at the end of the line,
At last, my friend will soon begin a new life intertwine.

So without any further delay, a grand toast to you.
A full course meal, and champagne or two.
Bloated and full with no room to explore,
Satisfied and swaddled we stroll to the dance floor.

We had such a blast but midnight passed.
Laughing and giggling, time track went by so fast.
Brimming with pride, I'm certain our friendship will last.
This beautiful bride with promises of high hope, faith and love.

Gina Hudgens

MY SONG BIRD

Song-sparrow, sing your rendition
Your whistles and trills got my attention,
Standing tall looking at your reflection
Is a glimpse, a broken image of rejection?

One woe your melancholy call
Screaming in silent helpless and all,
Even crows harsh voice drastically fall
No words utter, yet echoes in the wall.

You grow weary, dim and stubby
Fear and pain lurks unjustly,
Grievous wronged pierced tightly
Broken songs slander corruptly.

Behold, my tower of strength
You are more than that my dear friend,
Your courteous etiquette is heaven sent
Hearts of gold, a pure spirit descend.

Now, sing triumphantly sing
You persevere with angel's wing,
Endure love fit for a king
Your sweet melodious voice, celestial hymn.

FULLFILLMENT

God, you are the source of my well-being.

Repentance and redemption is my salvation.

Acceptance, and full surrender for my indifference.

The truth, and the path, to keep me in the right track.

Embracing my existence to trust you wholeheartedly.

Funneling all virtues, such happiness and amazing grace.

Undying flames that burn so bright, I thank you.

Life is your gift to me, Love is my gift to you, O Most High.

KINDNESS

It isn't hard to be kind. Open your heart and mind generously.
Accept people the way they are,
And give a lot of smiles.
After all, Life can Simply Be
Positively
Beautiful
Like
A
Sunbeam
Of

Rainbows

G.I.G.G.L.E.S

Smiles…………………………………

So………Infectious…………

Spread………..

Into…. A………TREE……OF……..

LAUGHTER ☺ ☺ ☺ AND ☺☺ ☺HAPPINESS.

PATRICIA CURRAN LOVE

Patricia Curran Love lives in Acton, California, with her husband, Chris, and writes a weekly educational column, "Sharpen, Brighten & Tighten," for the *Acton / Agua Dulce News*. Patricia minored in English Literature at USC and has a BFA, MA, and an Ed.S in Education. She taught Writing and Illustrating Children's Picture Books for several years at Learning Tree University.

She has authored several grants, including: a Job Training Partnership Act (JTPA), a Music Center Education Division Arts in the Schools for Los Angeles County Office of Education, and the California Urban Forests Council Newsletter (CUFC). She has edited and published student writing collections, including: *No Magi for Me* with L.A. Theater Works. She was a California State Writers' Project fellow at UCLA. Currently, she is finishing a collection of fairy tales: *Recollections of an Aging Carnivore*.

CHRISTMAS IN AUGUST

When my brother, Peter, was 12 and I was 17, I owned a 1951 MG TD. Early August, and it was a perfect day to ride in the classic sports car with fifteen coats of black lacquer, red tonneau cover, rolled down convertible top, candy red Naugahyde seats, dashboard with round metric English instruments, 4-speed stick shift in an H pattern, and a tiny back tool compartment in which two people could squish. The front of the car had a shiny chrome radiator with a hexagonal cap; white-walled wire-rim tires and a hubcap with MG pressed into the center.

The front window screwed down flat onto the two-sided hood; in this position, wind blew my long black hair straight back and bugs sometimes caught between our teeth. There was a square hole on the floor around the chrome accelerator pedal through which the road was visible. The absolute top speed was 75 MPH on level ground. Going up Angeles Crest, 35 was possible.

Everything was perfect that early afternoon, even the slight breeze. My brother and I drove down Honolulu to Ocean View in Montrose, California, singing loud and sweet, louder because the wind took the sound right out of our mouths. We sang *Silent Night, We Three Kings, Oh, Holy Night, and Oh, Tannenbaum.* The Great Christmas Spirit reigned within us and we were filled with Incredible Joy.

"Peace on the earth, good will to men,
from heaven's all-gracious King.
The world in solemn stillness lay,
to hear the angels sing!"

Peter and I were knowing true happiness at the moment we smacked into a parked truck on the side of the road.

The owner came running out of his house, dumbfounded, "You hit my truck and it was parked! What's wrong with you?" There was no damage to his truck or our sports car. We were going under 20 MPH.

"Merry Christmas!" we said, laughing, with tears running out of our eyes. We resumed our songs and feelings of good will. We were never happier. And the owner? He failed to see the beauty of it.

CHRISTOPHER E. LOVE

Christopher E. Love, award-winning writer and illustrator, lives in Acton, California with wife, Patricia. He has an undergraduate degree in journalism and graduate degrees in education. He worked as a free-lance feature writer for three daily newspapers in the mid 70s. In the 80s, as the Executive Art Director for a large publishing firm, he frequently published articles and illustrations for several magazines. His work appeared in *Air Progress, Military Modeler,* and *Combat Illustrated.* Mr. Love designed, wrote, and illustrated exhibition catalogs for the Los Angeles, Houston, and Arizona Auto Shows. He designed, edited, wrote articles, and created illustrations for the California Urban Forests Council, Zenith Insurance, and Acton COC newsletters. He currently writes and illustrates feature articles for the *Acton / Agua Dulce News.* Current projects include memoirs in short story form, two children's books, and a compilation of anomalous events in the Antelope Valley.

ERNIE AND CASPER

Morning light peeked through the curtains, teasing across Ernie's face. His eyes fluttered open. He lay there on his back and took in his surroundings. Home. A slow smile curled his lips.

He heard the thump, thump, thump of Casper's tail and glanced to the right. The little dog swam up the bed, nestling next to Ernie. His eyes sparkled and he made soft puppy-like sounds, in direct contrast to his graying muzzle. He shifted position several times as Ernie scratched behind his ears.

After a few moments Ernie sat up, swinging his feet to the floor, rolling his shoulders and arching his neck. He reached for the ever-present pack of cigarettes and lighter on the bedside table. Stepping into his slippers, he lit up the first smoke of the day, then ambled toward the bathroom to complete his morning routine.

Casper watched. When he was sure that Ernie was not coming right back, the compact canine stood up, moved higher on the bed, turned three times and put his head on the pillow. He went to sleep, snoring softly.

Ernie stood in the bathroom studying his reflection. The old man staring back at him had thinning, gray hair and white beard stubble. The nose seemed a bit large. His fingers traced the many scars on his chest, stopping at the still-healing place on the left side. He winced more from memory than pain. After two heart surgeries, and what they called, "a pacemaker procedure," his chest looked like a road map. He shook off the mood; it was not his nature to dwell. Instead, he picked up his razor and set to work.

Morning ritual finished, he returned to the bedroom. He slipped into gray pants, a matching work shirt, white socks and tennis shoes. He shooed Casper off the bed and made it. Casper, a tad indignant, trotted through the dog door to complete his morning ritual.

The old man gave the bedroom a swift check, and headed to the kitchen. He picked a well-seasoned cast-iron frying pan and lit the burner. An unmistakable slam let him know Casper was back, tail wagging, totally focused on what was coming.

"Do you want strawberry or grape jelly on your toast today?" Casper made a small growling noise. "Grape jelly it is!"

Coffee was already brewed. The rich aroma mingled with cigarette smoke in the air. Ernie threw several slices of bacon in the hot pan. It sizzled and popped as he concentrated on its crisping. Ernie always enjoyed making his own breakfast, even though it tired him out some days. The hospital never afforded him a chance to cook, or meals he considered palatable. At home, he always prepared food.

"It'll be ready soon, Casper."

He forked bacon onto the plate and cracked several eggs into the hot bacon grease. Soon the over-easy eggs joined the bacon. After a quick swipe with a butter-laden knife, toast was added. Ernie put their breakfast on the kitchen table, already set with utensils and a napkin. He filled a glass with cold, pulpy, orange juice. Finally, he poured himself a mug of coffee and added milk and sugar to make it drinkable.

Ernie broke off a small piece of toast and spooned a little jelly onto it. He tossed the morsel to his furry friend. The two companions ate mostly in silence, except for the smacking and licking of the dog's lips whenever the old man slipped him another portion. Casper's share tended to be substantial.

After breakfast, Ernie sat with a second cup of coffee and another cigarette. Casper waited by his side. The old man sat lost in thought as he gazed out the picture window that faced the back yard. He finished his coffee and said, "Shall we go outside for a while?"

A tapping tail answered his query. Ernie pocketed his cigarettes. The dishes could wait. On the way out he grabbed his prized chromatic harmonica. It was well-used and Ernie's "go-to" instrument.

He stepped through the sliding glass door as Casper banged through his dog door, and they met on the covered porch. Ernie sat in his favorite lounge chair and placed everything on a table beside him. The dog curled up on a small pillow next to the chair. His tail moved slowly. His eyes rarely left the old man.

Sunlight danced through the fruit trees and multicolored rose bushes. The air was rich with the scents of a spring garden. Ernie had planted and nurtured all the flora. It was hard to keep the garden up, so he had to delegate some of the work to a service. They did not love the yard as he did. It showed. He shook his head, then smiled as memories of trimming and planting flooded into his consciousness.

"I wish you could help me, Casper. I know we could make this yard a special place again. You would, if you could. I think, maybe, we're both getting a little too long in the tooth." He savored the fresh air then lit another cigarette, inhaling deeply. He blew a couple of smoke rings just for the fun of it.

Ernie stubbed out the cigarette, picked up his harmonica, and tapped it against the palm of his hand. He put it to his lips. The old man began to blow and draw gingerly, loosening the reeds. After a few minutes of riffing, he slipped into his favorite melody, *You Are My Sunshine*. The sweet, haunting sounds echoed under the patio cover and wafted into the yard.

Casper watched and listened intently, then lowered his head and went to sleep. Ernie continued to play one song after the other until he, too, felt weary. Putting the harmonica down, the old man leaned back in the lounge chair, closed his eyes and joined his friend in slumber. The wind, birds, and insects offered a perfect accompaniment to their soft snoring.

GOODBYE TO THE FISHERMAN

The old Mercury rolled north on what used to be US Route 66 from Bloomington to Streator, Illinois, a familiar one hour journey. We should have been bundled up and using the heater so late in the fall. We didn't need it. It was a mild morning, in the high 60s, almost unheard of on the last day of October.

A patchwork quilt of harvested fields was wrapped around remote farms and small towns as we traveled. The land reached out endlessly. Mountains, even hills, were non-existent in central Illinois. It was as if God had smoothed the land like a well-made bed. Teepees of corn stalks and piles of pumpkins, some carved with grotesque faces, emphasized the holiday along with the occasional scarecrow in someone's front yard.

Lisa, my younger sister, was the driver. She was used to big cars. She would have preferred her Lincoln Town Car to the twenty-five-year-old Woody station wagon. My mother and aunt sat in the back and I rode shotgun. The car belonged to Aunt Marie. My sister and I called her "Auntie Re." She was very protective of the ancient automobile, and Lisa counted herself lucky to be behind the wheel instead of my aunt.

The trip was a tightly woven mix of nostalgia and necessity. I marveled at the landscape. So many features had remained unchanged for more than thirty years. The roads, houses, farms, and businesses seemed identical to my mental scrapbook. It was as if I were a kid again, going to our family's summer campground.

Groaning a mild protest, the car angled down the same rough road it had traversed easily in its youth. The surrounding landscape and town had sidestepped the juggernaut of change. The campground had not. The signs announcing Lake Katchewan were new. The campground office was remodeled and pristine, a far cry from the ramshackle structure that served the purpose so long ago. We parked. Mom and I went in to speak with the site manager. He was dressed in a shirt and tie with black horn rimmed glasses and a name tag told us his name was Bill. The curmudgeonly ex-sheriff who ran the place in former times, Leonard, never needed a name tag. Everyone knew his name. Bill was just a kid, not old enough to have been born when my family camped there.

Mom explained we were visiting from California and used to camp and fish at the lake. Then she asked if we might take a look around, "For old time's sake."

Bill said it would be okay. He handed her a day pass. She thanked him and we walked back to the Woody. Lisa steered the car toward the main campground. We rolled the windows down, drinking in as much of the surroundings as possible. Water, trees, and dirt mingled scents. The faint aroma of fish evoked summers of days gone by.

We passed the lake, now surrounded by a chain-link fence and man-made beach. The white sand contrasted starkly with the murky, green water. The shore seemed better suited to a Hawaiian island. Rays of sunlight played across the water, sand, and fence. Two children were building a sand castle. No one was swimming. The water was too cold, despite the temperate day.

We passed the camping areas near the lake, now clearly victims of modernization, featuring cement pads, electrical hookups, barbecues and picnic tables. Shower and laundry facilities were only a short walk away. None of these conveniences existed before. Hamburgers were being grilled somewhere and the smell wafted in through the car's windows. I sighed. Mom did, too, almost in unison. I wondered if we had the same thought. I felt an incredible surge of loss. When old times entwine with what most people call progress, memory fades like threadbare cloth. The past welled up and I wiped my eyes.

Lisa guided the car onto the shadowy byway leading toward the nearby river. As we passed under the thick umbrella of trees, I closed my eyes and drifted. It was early July. I was sixteen again - young, strong, and invincible. My father and I slowly walked along the lane carrying backpacks full of fishing gear including open-face reels and trail poles, along with sodas and sandwiches. Dust, mixed with fog, had deposited droplets of muddy water on our tennis shoes. The morning haze swirled around our feet. The air carried an indefinable fragrance that only existed in summer. At the edge of the road, Diablo, our half timber-wolf canine companion, darted in and out of the undergrowth. We drank deeply of the still-cool air, knowing it would soon become heavy with the inevitable humidity of a Midwestern summer day. My father, Ernie, whistled his favorite song, *You Are My Sunshine*, and smoked an ever-present cigarette. His demeanor evoked a grown Tom Sawyer, right down to his straw hat and swagger. We were on the way to our fishin' hole.

Diablo was nowhere in sight, but I could hear him bounding through the thick woods. Dad and I reached the clearing where the lane ended. A series of narrow foot paths led to various spots on the river. One path crossed the river and ended at a hidden lake. That day, he chose to go down a path that led to my favorite fishing spot – a wide segment of the Vermillion River where we often found other bounty, including wild asparagus, watercress, berries, apples, and dandelion greens. The path was steep and treacherous. My father always seemed to revel in finding almost inaccessible fishing holes. He would laugh and point out that we never had to fight a crowd when we arrived. He was right. Sometimes solitude was the best part.

I was never afraid when my father was with me. His sinewy frame, hardened by a lifetime of arduous labor, had made him extremely tough. Dad and I always fished alone, since Mom and Lisa preferred to swim or go shopping in town. Sometimes we caught fish; many times we did not. Our time together was magical. We could sit in a boat, stand side by side on the bank, or wander half a mile apart searching for the ultimate trophy. The bond never wavered. Our souls fused when we put monofilament lines in the water.

I loved the smell of the river. The not-quite stagnant odor that emanated from the composting flora and fauna had always heightened my awareness of the abundance of life nearby. The gurgling rush of running water completed the scene. I was almost heady with the view. Crumbling and abandoned railroad trestle stanchions forded the river like the disembodied legs of giants. Piles of bricks at their bases afforded shelter from the current to bass, catfish, and bluegill. After a momentary pause to take it all in, we set to work assembling poles, attaching reels, adding hooks and bait. We each selected a likely spot and cast. The sunlight danced off our lines, making them glint like strands of a spider web. The two of us didn't speak during the preparation or fishing. We functioned as one, flowing with the river and forgetting the rest of the world for a too-short span of time.

The sun burned us. The wind buffeted us. An occasional thunderstorm drenched us. We swatted at passing insects as mosquitoes feasted on us. Fish fought us. We cast until our shoulders and arms throbbed with the effort. We quenched our thirst with warm soda and quelled our hunger with mangled sandwiches. We had the times of our lives. Diablo periodically left the woods to lay in an eddy-etched pool, cooling himself as he observed our efforts. After a while, bored, he returned to the forest.

When the sun dropped low in the sky, with or without fish, we followed the almost nonexistent trail back. Diablo ran circles around us, energized by the outing. Our legs ached and our lungs labored with effort in the early evening's humidity.

We always reached the clearing by twilight. Long shadows twisted across the road, offering a small measure of relief from the searing day. We were on our way back to the campsite, looking forward to a hearty dinner with Mom and Lisa. When Dad and I would return to the campsite, whatever was in season became part of the evening meal. In the absence of fish, the harvest would have constituted the entire feast if Mom hadn't packed steaks and hamburgers in the ice chest. A restful couple of hours by the campfire was punctuated by singing and storytelling, as the warm night blanketed us. Everyone enjoyed my father's harmonica accompaniment when we sang old songs. Days always ended with a deep sleep. Mornings brought new adventures. Weekends ended all too soon.

The car stopped. The past was gone with a jerk and the squeal of worn brakes. I looked at the others. Everyone sat in silence for a long moment.

Mom finally spoke, "Kit, we want you to do this. No one can make it except you," she said solemnly, as she handed me the simple box containing my father's ashes.

She, as did all of my immediate family, called me Kit. It was my great grandfather's nickname, handed down to me. Long ago I had become Chris to everyone, even my wife, Pat. Still, there at that time, it seemed essential that I become Kit again. My mother and aunt were far too old to travel on foot down the steep trails. Lisa was not well and could not join me. Dad and I would travel to the river together for the last time, leaving "Da Wimmin," as he called them, behind.

I tried to locate one of the trails we had used so many years ago. After careful searching, I finally discovered the hint of a path and took it. The bank seemed steeper and more complex than I remembered. In several places, I had to brush aside spider webs. The trail had been unused for a long time. It would have been reassuring to hear Diablo crashing through the undergrowth. After a while, sweating and breathing heavily, I was at the river. The rich, loamy scent of the wet earth mingled with my own. I inhaled deeply.

The unmistakable bouquet of the river hadn't changed. I studied the legs of the giants; time had diminished them.

Near the water's edge, I opened the small box and scattered my father's ashes along the bank and over the water. They melded and disappeared almost instantly. We were together in a spot that I had believed lost to us forever. This had been the right thing to do.

Hearing a soft rustling in the woods, I whispered, "Hello Diablo, Dad's finally come back to keep you company."

I stood on the river bank in the mists of remembrance and lingered, unmoving, for an unmeasured interim. Dive-bombing insects brought me back to the present. I watched an iridescent dragonfly dart across the river toward the hidden lake and slowly turned my back on the water.

I felt a sense of completion. Mom and Lisa were waiting at the top. I had been at the river longer than I thought. Long shadows indicated the day was waning. We stood silently, hugged, then climbed into the car. Aunt Marie waited, clearly undone by the circumstances. The station wagon groaned down the lanes and out of the campground. Lisa guided the old Woody toward the highway. Glancing back toward Lake Katchewan, I wished I'd brought my fishing gear.

MARY DENNING

Mary Denning, an eleven year resident of the Quartz Hill section of the Antelope Valley, is a native of Southern California where she and husband Joe raised their six children. She is a graduate of California State University Northridge with a degree in Art. Her artwork has been exhibited and sold at galleries in Cambria, Santa Cruz, and the San Fernando Mission, where she currently has a painting on display as part of their art collection.

After retiring from her job with the Los Angeles Library System, Mary decided to try her hand at writing. Her first attempt won her recognition in a local newspaper. She now enjoys writing short stories and poetry, and was recognized by the City of Palmdale for winning their inaugural "Walk On Words" poetry contest. Mary recently published a children's book, *The Sunflower Story*, which she has both written and illustrated.

THE MORNING LIGHT

Awaken Sun and goodnight moon
As darkened skies depart quite soon
Then gently morning light appears
When peeking on horizon's spheres
And softly glows on mountain peaks
Where sun and shade play hide and seek
And rays of sun descend the heights
Where iridescent shades delight
Brilliant hues of copper gold
Covering all in its path tenfold
And warming desert sands it seeks
To mystify and be unique

SEA SHELLS AND ROLLER SKATES

Beach promenade awaits

Enjoyment there for all your sakes

Merry-go-round and innocent thrills

Ocean piers and fishing skills

Favorite restaurants

With the best of mates

Shooting stars and romantic dates

Chocolate cake and barbecued steaks

Cotton candy and side-show fakes

Summer nights and silver lakes

Butterflies and honeysuckle

Lemonade and children's chuckles

Lightning bugs and water ripples

Moonlight dancing

And harmless romancing

Sailboats and summer winds

Fond memories that begin

of summer days so long ago

but never lost to the love I know

Yesterdays have gone away

Tomorrows bring uncharted days.

BARNEY GOOGLE

He had a coat of reddish brown
His kindly eyes were small and round
Ancestry questioned can't be found
Barney Google was his name
Entertaining was his game
Fighting rocks became his fame

When children laughed he loved it best
The bigger the crowd the better the test
Even birds flocked from their nests
Encouraged by applause he never rests

He tackled rocks as large as he
Snarling, barking, fierce as can be
Immobile rocks might like to flee
But Barney showed no mercy there
T'was dog to rock in this warfare

Soon Barney wore his dentures down
Deterring not his fierceness found
Renowned beyond his circle bound
His fame lived on beyond his years
And tales were told while drinking beers
Of great times had while children cheered
Ole Barney's missed we've shed our tears
Now Angels laugh when he appears.

ANGELS IN OUR LIVES

Some years back when traveling to Costa Rica, I had the good fortune of meeting my daughter-in-law Flori's family. They are lovely people, family oriented and humble, generous, and kind by nature. Flori's sister, Cecilia, has spent her adult life helping the poor. Every day she visits the local orphanage distributing clothes and food that she collects from neighbors. She is also a kidney donor. Her life has not been easy, but Cecilia finds time each day to visit her widowed father to bring him his daily meals. So I'm not surprised that an angel would enjoy visiting Cecilia. Yes, I do believe there are angels.

Cecilia is the mother of four living children, two girls and twin boys, Michael and Joshua. Cecilia's oldest son died at an early age. When Michael was fifteen, he discovered a growth on his abdomen. His brother, Joshua, advised him that he must inform their mother. Aware then of this hazard to his health, she immediately made a doctor appointment. It was a rare cancer and they needed to operate at once. While at the hospital for preparations for the surgery, they met the two doctors who would perform the operation. One doctor had a great and kind bedside manner and became a friend to Michael and Cecilia. Before the surgery he assured Michael that he would be okay. Michael came through it fine and his new friend was by his side to comfort him while he recovered in the hospital.

When Michael was fully recovered, he and Cecilia came back to the hospital with a thank-you gift for this especially kind doctor. They inquired at the nurses station for the doctor who had spent so much time with Michael. The nurses did not know of that doctor, but did inquire throughout the hospital if anyone knew of him. No one did. They asked the other doctor who did the surgery where they could locate this other doctor. He said there was no other doctor with him.

Some years later when Michael came to visit me I questioned him about this mystery. He said they had tried for many years to locate him with no avail. No one knew of him. Michael said that he was so very kind and good that there could be no other answer except that he was an angel. "He came to us and blessed our lives forever."

I believe there must be angels all around us. Sometimes helping us in many ways we never notice. A lost letter is found in a place we looked before, or an accident is avoided by mere seconds. How many times has each of us been protected, unaware of the angels in our own lives?

HANDS

Beautiful unique tools that only we possess
Created and blessed
And given with tenderness
How we use them speaks words to impress
Loving Mothers use them to caress

Sometimes Fathers use them to correct
Often they are used with great effect
Communicating tools we choose to select

Throughout this world we've been advised
To use these tools when it applies
Sergeants demand a correct reply
And greetings call for a cheerful high-five

Policemen use them in the street
Drummers use them to keep the beat
Tightrope walkers steady their feet
Conductors control music with hands that sweep
Pantomimes hands are actors unique
Fingers that write most everyone seeks
Surgeons' hands bless those they meet

Graceful and noble solely to each soul
Hands are the gift from God alone.

SOARING

Up above the Desert skies
World renowned and famous fly
Hypersonic rocket-powered
Test pilot speeds empowered
World Record breaking flights
Reaching incredible heights
Blackbird flies the fastest
According to the lastest

Pilots now do seek new quests
Never looking for a rest
Always wanting to do their best
Leads to world renowned progress
Mojave Desert enterprise
Rocket Science is so wise
Seeking unknown skies around
Atmospheres that have no bounds

WATERMELON WINE

Reminiscing about those good old days

And sharing stories of our daring ways

Of adventures taken when we were young

Memories shared and favorite songs sung

And looking back we recalled what was good

Watermelon wine drank with friends we knew

Laughing over foolish things done in our pasts

And making Watermelon wine in large casks

And those poker games when we were just teens

And cul-de-sac baseball games played when fifteen

And building forts in eucalyptus trees

With carpet samples and some of Mom's things

Unknown to Mom her silver set the scene

Lemon grove fights fought with lemons and glee

And taking Mom's old Honda on a spree

Another cause for Mom to disagree

And surfing days at Zuma riding waves

And college days when there's no time to play

Great friends we've known and kept through the years

Being there for graduations, joys and tears

Remembering all that was good and dear.

Mary Denning

A MOTHER'S LOVE

Before sunrise she awakes
Readying her children for their sakes
Healthy breakfasts she does make
Then packing lunches for each to take
Checking that the clothes they wear
Are clean and bright as she declares
Hugs and kisses off they go
Cheerfully to school so they should know
Education and learning is not woe

A Mother's Love is always there
Throughout our lives she is prepared
To motivate and understand
To discipline and give acclaim
Giving encouragement first hand
Her delight in them is grand
Throughout their lives her heart will share
Success and failures with their welfare
For a Mother's Love is always there.

KATIE RYAN

Katie Ryan lives in the picturesque hills and canyons of Green Valley, which is perfect for her love of horses. It's in her blood as she grew up in Minnesota on a farm and always around horses. Her father, an avid horseman, once rode the Continental Divide on horseback along with the governor of Minnesota. Katie became a licensed therapist in California with degrees from Antioch University and Phillips Graduate Institute, and found a way to help heal others using horses through equine therapy. She is EAGALA certified.

Katie recently combined her love of horses and family with her talent for writing and published *Horse Wisdom Alchemy*, a book that derives its title from her therapy business. Part memoir and part educational, her book is a collection of 100 years of horse stories, all true. Katie currently is applying her writing skills to the motion picture industry to produce a documentary, *Coyote*, about cowboy singer Don Edwards.

THE MONTH OF MAY

It is the calm before the storm or the push before the big heat.

The lilacs have nearly dried up but the evergreens have new piney shoots.

The hills have lush different shades of green.

The end of May brings Memorial Day – a day to remember those we have lost to war, or loved ones that have gone on before.

Only this May I will remember my Mother because she is still here.

When I think of her I think how loving and caring she is. Whenever a fire, flood, or earthquake is reported on the news I get a call from a soft-spoken lady who asks if I'm okay.

I joke that I pray for disasters because I know I will hear from her.

She has lived an incredible life. She has more talent than most. She was a teacher of Music, Humanities, and English. She was the organist at our church and would accompany choirs singing the "Hallelujah Chorus."

She can draw and paint and still does difficult crossword puzzles. I have always looked up to her and still do.

We had a party several years back and all my Mother's watercolors were on display thanks to my sister, for the partygoers celebrating our barn being 100 years old.

My Mother brought class and grace to my parents' farm with her Swedish simplicity, from hanging a picture or adding a pillow.

At ninety-four she can still play her piano and I cherish every letter she sends me.

My Mother is the month of May.

THE SOLDIER
(an excerpt from *Horse Wisdom Alchemy*)

There are several treatment strategies for dealing with patients who have had trauma. However, dealing with the military can be difficult as many clinicians do not have the training to deal with the multi-faceted issues that may be present

I had always thought that animal-assisted therapy would be the right fit for soldiers coming back. You can have various trainings in order to be more prepared in dealing with veterans but unless you have been a soldier yourself it's pretty hard to even scratch the surface of what these people have been through. When I got the opportunity to work with some veterans I jumped at the chance to introduce the horses.

Our soldier, Eric, came to a session in the arena because he had recently lost two close friends in Afghanistan in the line of duty and wanted to work through some of the grief and loss. He was willing to allow us to tell his story.

Eric entered the arena and was given a bucket with paper labels displaying the five stages of grief: Bargaining, Denial, Depression, Anger, and Acceptance, in no particular order. There was also a label with "ME" written on it and "Friend." There were five horses to choose from including an older mini horse who was slightly limping.

The first horse Eric labeled was Denial, placed on a large Paint. He placed Depression on an older white horse. He mentioned that "denial" and "depression" are around all the time. He attempted to attach Acceptance onto an older brown horse but the brown horse ran off.

Eric gingerly placed "Friend" on another white horse that he said represented his friend that had died. Finally he got down on his knees and place the "ME" label on the mini which he called "the wounded warrior." Tears were flowing.

He was then asked to build his world using the props, and he built a representation of his family including someone who had abused him. The horse knocked it over and the white horse (Friend) stayed by his side. Suddenly Depression and Denial literally walked to the gate, unlocked it with their mouths, and left the arena. All that remained were "ME," "Friend," and "Acceptance." Someone once said, "You can't make this stuff up!"

STEVE ORDWAY

Steve Ordway is a retired fireman who lives in Leona Valley. His honorable career as a fireman with the Los Angeles City Fire Department spanned twenty-five years, twelve of which were spent as a paramedic on an ambulance. He had the unusual distinction of being the only paramedic firefighter when the department assimilated the civilian paramedic ambulance personnel from the central receiving hospital. Due to manpower shortages during this changeover, Steve was detailed to work on a rescue ambulance most of his assigned shifts. These assignments were almost always in South Central Los Angeles or Hollywood.

Steve's wife encouraged him to write down his many experiences responding to emergency calls. He has written over one hundred tales, some funny, some gory (as is the nature of the job), and all dealing with the day to day life of a fireman. He hopes to compile these stories into a book.

SITTING ON GO – LIFE AT THE FIRE FACTORY

When watching me eat, people often remark, "I can see that you learned to eat fast at the fire station, before an alarm interrupted your dinner." In truth, my whole family and I gobbled down meals. I was slow compared to my brother, Sid. He was twelve years old before he learned what the word 'chew' meant. Firemen do pound down the vittles quickly. I suppose my family's eating habits helped in one way to prepare me for my future career.

Living while 'sitting on go' does take some adjustment. We all learned that showering must be done in increments. Shampoo, then rinse, lather upper body, then rinse, and so on. Wearing a head full of shampoo to a brush fire is miserable. When you start to sweat, and you will sweat while hauling the hose up the hill, the soap runs into your eyes, stinging and blinding you. When you finally get the empty line into position and it's loaded, you'd look rather silly dousing yourself. Toilet protocol also required a particular routine, especially having your 'paperwork' prepared as Step 1.

If you're doing station maintenance in the back of the station or the side yard, or anywhere that you might not hear an alarm, you'd better notify one of your buddies. My greatest fear was that I might miss a run. I have bad dreams, even today after years of retirement, that I'm at the station and miss a run. A good friend that I worked with for many years, and is also long retired, told me that he has the same dream.

At night, firemen have their canvas turnout pants pushed down around their tall rubber boots next to their beds. When the alarm comes in they stick their stocking feet in the boots, pull up their pants putting suspenders over shoulders, and throw on their jackets while heading for the fire pole. A fireman's turnout coat and helmet is on the rig. It became so automatic after a while that I once slid the pole, got on the tailboard, donned my coat, and was putting on my helmet when I was awakened by the truck starting to leave. I almost fell off.

When riding the rescue ambulance, you must respond in uniform, not turnouts (protective clothing). I would push my uniform pants down around my zippered leather boots, and I had my white shirt on the rescue room door knob. I was able to respond quickly due to practice. It's not unusual to have three rescue runs after midnight, each of which will cost you an hour of sleep. Due to those years of sleep deprivation, today I can fall asleep hanging over the back of a chair.

The routine at a fire station consists of duties which are laid out on a daily basis:

MONDAY: windows and screens
TUESDAY: lawn, driveway, parking area
WEDNESDAY: mop and wax floors
THURSDAY: brass polishing. This includes the fittings on the rigs, brass poles, and door knobs. Older stations had brass plumbing under the sinks, brass hand plates on doors, and dedication plaques in front of the building.
FRIDAY: refrigerator, stove, kitchen area.
SATURDAY and SUNDAY: performing drills with hose lays, ladder evolutions, and other equipment.

In multiple company houses work is divided up by company. For example: Engine Company gets the front half of the station (officers' quarters, kitchen, study room); Truck Company gets the rear of the station (locker room, bath and shower room, dormitory). The apparatus operators are responsible for their rig's appearance and equipment, plus sweeping and mopping the apparatus floor.

Other regular duties include: hose and hydrant testing, fire prevention, hose cleaning and changing, plus basic station maintenance. If the station has a steady cook, he is a god, and as such, is exempt from all duties.

When annual inspection rolls around all participate in wall and ceiling light washing. Many wooden ladders and tool handles require refinishing. This involves scraping, sanding, and varnishing.

The firehouse relationship is that of a band of brothers. We share each other's plans, thoughts, and hopes. Family life and problems are openly discussed, and advice, some good and some bad, is freely given. Our families come to the station on holidays when we are assigned to work them. And we all party together when we don't have to work them. We turn out in mass at a crew member's house to help with building or other projects. For one third of our lives we live side by side. We operate at emergencies together where we depend on each other, and we experience the same horror, sadness, and elation that these incidents produce.

To relieve tension, we joke with each other. Trash day always tickled me when the call would go out over the P.A. system, "Can a man, man a can." The best laughs I've ever had have been at the fire factory, usually at someone's expense. This humor is exhibited in many of my stories. In short, we are very close.

The worst of times are when one of the guys is trapped, and you have to try and rescue him. It's tough when a crew member is injured, and devastating when someone is killed in the line of duty. The hardest story I ever wrote was about when we lost one of our firemen while responding to an emergency. His name was Dominic Pascal, and I will never forget him.

CLOSE CALL

In firefighting there are different jobs for different companies. Engine companies have the hose and pump the water. Enginemen, or 'engies,' go into the burning buildings and put out the fire. Truck companies carry ladders, axes, and forcible entry tools. These truckmen, or 'truckies,' provide entry for the engies, do search and rescue, and cut the electrical wires. But their main duty is to provide ventilation.

When the smoke is so thick that you can't see your flashlight in front of your mask, let alone your hand, fire suppression is difficult. You pull the hose blindly down the hallway, hoping that there's not a hole in the floor just ahead waiting to swallow you up. This is when you pray that a truckie will soon cut a hole in the roof, break out windows and clear out the smoke.

Ventilating a roof is the most dangerous operation in structure fire fighting. A good truckie will know that first you ladder at the corner of the building, if possible. You want the end of the ladder to extend six to eight feet above the parapet wall. This makes it much easier to find in smoky conditions if a hasty retreat from the roof is necessary. It's paramount that all firefighters know how to walk the roof. They must know where it's strong and where it's weak, and be able to spot signs of failing. When the protruding pipes seem to be getting longer this means that the roof is sagging, and shiny areas indicate that heat is melting the tar. Most important is where and how to cut the hole, and then quickly get off the roof once that's accomplished.

We were called to a Thrifty Drug Store fire. The building was fully involved as our task force arrived as part of a greater alarm assignment. Our truck was ordered to the roof. The aerial ladder was raised and up went the truckies with their axes and chain saw, knowing that this roof was weak due to the time that the fire had been burning. I followed with a protection line.

I was at the middle of the ladder when the roof started going in. All of the truckies crowded back onto the ladder with me. One even leaped off and caught the side of the aerial like a trapeze act.

As he swung underneath, I reached through the rungs and grabbed the straps of his breathing apparatus. With the help of the other firemen, we pulled him to safety. That was when someone asked, "Where's Larry?" Six-foot, four-inch Larry was not in sight. We hastily descended the ladder because the flames were now shooting up, licking at its end.

Good Lord, what a sinking feeling in my gut at the realization that we had lost him. But I was quickly relieved, hearing the words, "There he is!"

Around the corner, protruding out from the wall about ten inches was the Thrifty Drug sign, and perched atop it on his tippy toes was Larry, his size fourteen boots lacking a foot hold. He was crouching below the parapet, trying to make himself shorter. We quickly put a ladder up to the sign and rescued him.

CHIHUAHUA

It was a chilly fall evening at Fire Station 93. It happened that the rear parking lot of the station shared a common chain link fence with the Ventura Freeway. During the nine years that I was assigned there, I experienced a few traffic accidents that occurred directly behind the station.

The sun had just set when an aging Hispanic man's jalopy broke down and came to rest on the right shoulder of the freeway. A highway patrol officer parked behind the disabled clunker with his yellow lights blinking. The old man wore a heavy overcoat. His long gray hair bushed out from under his broad brimmed black hat. In broken English, he tried to explain his situation to the officer. All the while he was sheltering his little Chihuahua that peeked out from the front of his coat. The officer radioed for a tow unit which, upon arrival, parked behind the Highway Patrol car.

Even though traffic was light at that time of the day, a distracted driver managed to rear end the tow truck, sending it over the embankment into a ditch. This same car then caromed across the freeway and collided with another vehicle, effectively blocking all four lanes. Soon other motorists joined the fray - crashing, spinning, and one even overturning, ending up on its roof.

From within the fire station we heard the collisions. We responded quickly and found a dozen smashed vehicles. Numerous people were injured. Fuel was leaking from one of the cars and the smell of gasoline permeated the area, but we were able to get water on it before it ignited.

In all, five rescue ambulances, two additional engine companies, and six more CHP units arrived on scene. The injured were treated and transported from the now closed Ventura Freeway. Tow units from all over the San Fernando Valley arrived and began clearing up this demolition derby. By the time the tow truck was winched from the ditch we had finished picking up our hose. We departed with the last remaining CHP units on our heels, thus reopening the freeway.

I noticed that watching us leave was this old Hispanic man. He was standing in the darkness next to a broken down jalopy, with the nose of his little Chihuahua peeking out from the front of his coat

HAPPY CHIEF

"OCD from Engine 93, we have a loom up, let the whole assignment come through," I radioed while responding toward the tower of smoke.

"Roger 93's, you're getting delayed assistance from outside the area," replied the OCD (Operations Control Division). With the Division Evaluation Drill going on that day, all the nearest companies were unavailable.

Stanley, our most veteran fireman, hooked the hose around the hydrant, and we 'laid a line' down the street. The rear portion of the house was well involved with fire. We were faced with protecting the neighbor's house and the garage, both of which were exposed and were starting to burn. We also needed to attack the fire before the entire structure became involved. With just one other fireman, Joe, and the Engineer, Lumpy, who drives and operates the pump, plus myself as the acting Captain, we were short on manpower and help would be delayed.

I took an inch and a half line to protect the adjoining home and Joe took another one to protect the garage. Stanley, hooking up and loading the hose at the hydrant, wouldn't be available right away and by then the fire would spread throughout the house.

"Battalion 17 on scene," crackled the radio as the Chief's red and white sedan pulled up. Recognizing our dilemma, Chief Durkee told his driver to pop the trunk as he exited the car. He then grabbed his brand new, never used, bright white turnout coat and helmet from within and quickly donned them. The Chief then grabbed a breathing apparatus and hose line off our apparatus.

A muffled "Yabba Dabba Du" was heard from his face mask as the Chief, resplendent in his gleaming white attire, charged through the front door. It was his first chance to fight a fire since he made Chief many years before. Imagine their surprise when the second company arrived and the firemen bringing in their backup line saw who they were relieving.

Out from the smoky house came the Battalion Chief sporting a blackened helmet and coat, soggy pants, and dirty boots. He wasn't pretty anymore, but he had a huge smile on his face.

ELAINE BROWN

Elaine Brown found her way to the Antelope Valley from her childhood home of Ontario, Canada, where memories of her grandmother reading her children's classics instilled a love of storytelling. She honed her early writing skills by composing letters to friends in distant cities. Later after raising four daughters, she entered the work force as an Executive Assistant, a position that educated her in the short, tight writing requirements of the engineering field.

Throughout the years, Elaine's desire to write fiction grew. She took various creative writing courses, but it was her enrollment in an online course with the Long Ridge Writers Group that really pushed her to challenge herself. Now retired, Elaine has more time to devote to writing. She composes short fiction and hopes to branch out into longer efforts. Her co-authors are her ever-present canine desk mates: Mimi, Precious and Chiqui.

SILVER QUEEN
Against night velvet
The silver queen floats with grace
Among the mountain peaks

ICE FANTASY
Ice laden branches
Glisten in crystal brilliance
Enchanting the senses

ROSE GARDEN
Rose garden blooms
Fragrant, serene, colorful
Warming the spirit

MOONLIT GARDEN
Moonlight paints silver
Caressing petals in garden
Romancing the heart

SUMMERS IN CANADA

Memories of summers on my grandparents' island at Honey Harbour, Ontario, Canada still bring me joy and peace decades after my last visit there. This beautiful island, no more than about four acres, was shaped more or less like a bent dumb bell. The back bay on the lea side of the island protected our boats, and when the water level was low sported a soft sand beach. The opposite side of the island faced west and granite rock sloped to the water's edge. Our island was only one of the thirty-thousand islands dotting the Canadian side of Lake Huron known as Georgian Bay. Honey Harbour is about 100 miles north of Toronto up Highway 400.

My grandparents purchased the island from the Crown shortly after their marriage sometime at the turn of the century. They had some local Huron Indians build a log cabin on it. I barely remember a shallow lean-to kitchen off one side that my grandfather built. Some years later, he attached a large kitchen to the log cabin where for years family members gathered around the large table. This kitchen had five good sized windows giving a view to the forested areas at the back and the back bay at the front.

I was told that in the early years there was a boat house on the bay. However, the winter current and ice ruined it. My grandfather had the boat house shell pulled up on the rocky area overlooking both the back bay and front side of the island. He lined it with cedar stripping. It was left as an open area with only curtains to create privacy. Windows on three sides of this sleeping cottage, allowed a cooling breeze to flow through. It was from the screened porch of this dwelling that I first saw the stunning Northern Lights way off on the horizon on an evening shortly before returning back home to Windsor to start another year of school.

In those early years there was no electricity or plumbing or regular toilets on the island or anywhere in the local vicinity. They had candles and oil lamps for the evening light, but usually we went to bed early and rose early. Water was kept in a tin pail and kept fairly cool when placed in the west side window. There was an old wooden icebox kept cold with blocks of ice purchased from a vendor in the harbor. He stored blocks of ice from the winter's frozen lake.

In those days the water was so clean we could drink it right out of the lake without boiling it first. All that changed later with the coming of more people and speed boats to the area. There was nothing quite like the trip down the path to what my grandparents called the Parliament building - the two-seater outhouse. Of course, no one wanted to make that trip in the night, so there were pots under the beds. I'm so glad the days of those pots are over! Laundry was done in huge tubs using a wash board. It was rinsed in the lake and hung on lines strung around trees. Cooking was done on the old iron wood stove in the corner of the kitchen.

Eventually, electricity was run through the islands and mainland. My grandmother never did forgive the hydro company for disfiguring the beauty of her island by cutting a swath of trees down the whole length to string their lines. My grandfather had an electrician come and bring electricity into the dwellings. There were many outlets, but some were covered with tape to prevent an overload. Grandfather also purchased a length of wide hose and a pump that ran from the front of the island to the kitchen sink. So now it was no longer necessary to carry pails of water from the lake. Much later a bathroom was built off the side of the kitchen accessible from outside. About that same time, a wringer washing machine was introduced to the island.

As a child, I ran barefoot over some of the island being careful to avoid the many patches of poison ivy that my mother and grandmother tried in desperation to kill. It's hard to say just what was my favorite thing about the island and about the area. There were so many wonderful things I enjoyed there. Year after year I won the row boat races at the regatta in the harbor with my grandparents' old English skiff. She was a light craft that I could make dance over the water. For a number of years, it was my only way to travel to visit friends at other cottages. My favorite boat is still a canoe because it can travel into places others can't.

I loved the trees - fragrant pine and cedar, birch, oak, maple and more. I loved the granite rocks and boulders where I could sit for hours and look out over the water at the changing weather patterns - the glorious Canadian sunsets, a wall of rain coming in, or just be in the presence of the majesty surrounding me. I never gave that activity a name, but I think it was simple meditation. It's where I learned to love to be alone with nature.

Most summer days were gentle days with fairly calm winds and waves. But the area could be quite deceiving. There were days when we suffered three day blows where it was dangerous to take small boats out into the open water fronting our island. On these days, my grandmother made bread in the wood stove. Oh yes, the fragrance of that baking bread was divine.

Sometimes we had to rescue people whose boats capsized at the front of the island. Usually these were young people in canoes, part of large camps who had just traversed the back waterways not realizing what was in store for them when they hit the open water. It was and is important to know the water levels and just where you should and shouldn't drive your motor boats in that area as there are many shoals just below the water that can shear the motor pins. One such shoal is off the far end of our island and on low water level years it can just barely be seen, and sometimes even the row boat would just skim the surface.

I learned to swim in that back bay, but was always careful to cruise the surface of the water when swimming out further into the bay because of the forest of water weeds that grew thick there. These rubbery weeds could pull a swimmer under if a person got caught in them. During the years when I was training on my high school swim team, I would swim the distance between the island and the nearby mainland. One can no longer do that because of the increased boat traffic.

Another of the things I loved about being on the island was the quiet afternoons when I was still quite young, when I would lie beside my grandmother and listen to her read to me the classic children's books. She made the characters come alive for me.

Fishing was an activity I learned early. In those early days, there was a system where people were on a schedule to bring mail from the post office out to the islands and cottages. A shingle-covered wooden box was placed on a dock pretty much central to those who received mail. On many occasions on our way to pick up mail, my grandmother would row the boat, and I would feed out a troll line with a spinner hook on it from the back of the boat. I often caught a good sized lake pike. Since I was informed that if I wanted to share in eating the fish, I had to clean it, I learned pretty fast how to prepare the fish after it was hung to dry.

My grandfather would take me year after year up to a ridge on the mainland to pick blueberries. Not every year was a good year for them. But on the good years it didn't take long to fill the tin pails. My grandmother would make us blueberry pancakes and pies and jam. At the beginning of July, I could find a few very tasty wild strawberries, but never enough to do anything with except to enjoy on the spot.

On some lazy days, I'd lie in the old canvas hammock on the front porch of the log cabin and swing for hours. On other days, I'd roam the island. Sometimes I'd spend time at a place on the island where the rock was shaped like a large slanted couch and just make believe stories about that rock. Sometimes I'd gather the foam at the water's edge and make believe stories about how I would use it. I loved to collect stones - different colors, shapes, sizes. I especially liked the clear quartz.

I was part of a bunch of young people who vacationed there every year. Dorothy, Hannah, Peter, John and Sue and I enjoyed getting together to swim, play, take boat trips to the harbor to enjoy banana splits and eventually dances. One year after winning many races at the regatta, some of us decided to go for a swim out to Brandon's Island about two miles away from our cottage. Sue rowed my skiff, while Dorothy, Peter, and I swam the distance. I was the only one who was in training for swimming, so I kept swimming out and back to them. We sure got in trouble for doing that without adult supervision.

We didn't have a sail boat, but it was always fun to watch the sail boat races that circled around one of the large islands just west of ours. It was just another of the beautiful sights of the area.

There was a Canadian artist, Tom Thompson, who was famous in Canada for painting scenes of the Canadian North and wild Algonquin Park with the rocks and wind-bent trees. His paintings reminded me of our island.

So much of that beauty and experience was taken for granted while I was growing up. The island is no longer owned by our family, but my memories are so ingrained they are a very real part of me - a bitter sweet part of me. I am ever so grateful for having lived that life and enjoyed God's country for so many years.

Elaine Brown

THE SPIRIT OF KAUAI

Aloha!

Come, journey with me into the spirit and rhythm that is Kauai. Can you hear it, feel it; the heavy pulse of the endless ocean that booms and reverberates like distant cannons in its relentless assault on this ancient shore? Palm trees, grasses, and countless varieties of flora bend and dance to the cadence of the Trade Winds.

Can you smell the fragrance of spice that rises from the ground cover beside our path on the ocean bluff? Press a waxy petal of the red torch ginger plant between your finger tips. Sniff the exotic scent of the yellow centered white Plumeria blossom that we pick up from the lawn beneath its flower laden tree.

Let us remove our shoes and feel the sand under our feet, and let the cool water lap over them as we stand on a golden beach. Let us enjoy the harmony and oneness of water, sand, breeze and fragrance that is Kauai. Imagine the sway of the Hula dance by young men and women on this sun-warmed beach as they bend to the rhythm and beat of drums and guitars in imitation of the spirit of Kauai. Hear and learn the melody and harmony of their words and music as it drifts on the tropical breeze.

Cotton ball clouds float above and create moving shadows upon the earth. Without warning, it rains warm and refreshing upon us. Look, in the distance there is a rainbow, now a double rainbow in jeweled hues. In moments the rain will pass.

Come away again to the path through a sultry and scented forest that boasts many shades of green in varied shapes, sizes, and textures. Pull a guava fruit from a tree and savor its sweet exotic flavor. Although we cannot see them, we hear the raucous sounds of birds that hide in the dense foliage. Now and then we come across several of the numerous wild and colorful hens that inhabit this island. Here is a group of them pecking the ground at the foot of a many aerial-rooted Banyan tree.

We find ourselves at the foot of the fern grotto high above us. The sky is barely visible as we raise our faces to view the narrow waterfalls that plunge many feet between the ferns and flora dripping from the cliff side.

Our path takes us back to the shrub-lined river. We wave to the kayakers. Let us board a tour boat to return to the ocean shores.

We are entertained by the smooth island music and the beauty of a woman who dances a slow musical and romantic story told in the undulated movement of hands, arms, body, and eyes.

The sun is nearing the western horizon. It infuses rose, coral, lavender, and red hues upon the canvas of sky, ocean, and land. We are beckoned to come join the crowd of people attending a luau. We are greeted warmly. A lei of welcome, a mixture of white and purple Plumeria, is arranged about our necks. Here we are treated to the flavors of roast pig, beef, and chicken, spiced and herbed to tempt the palate. There is a large bowl of tropical fruit. We heap our plates from the many mysterious and aromatic dishes presented, then take our seats.

Look to the stage. The dancers have assembled and music has begun for our entertainment. Many island stories are related in the various dances and songs. The finale is a wild fire dance that excites the night.

We leave to find our rest, and to dream of the spirit and rhythmic motion that is Kauai.

Mahalo for coming on this trip with me.

Aloha!

MELINDA M. HUNTER

A native of Chicago, Melinda Hunter moved to the Antelope Valley in 2010. An active member of the Antelope Valley Writers Association, Melinda is also active in her church, and sings in the Antelope Valley Master Chorale. She holds a B.A. in English from Carleton College and an M.Div. (Master of Divinity) from North Park Seminary in Chicago..

Melinda has been writing poetry since the age of five, and has the amazing ability of reciting all of her early poems from memory. Her poem, "October's Voice," received a prize in the Iowa State Poetry contest, and her article, "The Lady Who Slew a Thousand Dragons," was published in *Faith and Inspiration* magazine. She is a prolific poet and also enjoys writing haiku and short stories, particularly using animals as characters or inventing her own creatures.

RAIN

I remember rain
in Illinois.
It floods the streets
and the basements
There are even boats
on the streets
Now lakes.

I remember rain
in the Antelope Valley.
I see cumulus clouds
full to bursting.
Finally,
they disburse a drop
Or two.

SPRING

Spring springs sprightly,
Oh so lightly.
Overnightly
She turns green.

What a lady!
She's not shady,
Sister Summer
Is that Queen.

Up come flowers,
And there're showers.
Longer hours
Reign supreme.

There are hues,
Greens and blues,
Spread the news:
Spring can be seen.

OCTOBER'S VOICE

October's voice is calling me
I cannot help but follow.
Down little, winding forest paths
That lead to Gypsy Hollow.

I smell the campfire's fragrant smoke
And bubbling, savory stew.
The gold and scarlet leaves I see
And glorious sky of blue.

As I ascend the rocky path
My heart is wild and free.
I camp beside the gurgling stream
The glittering stars I see.

As on my bed of boughs I lie
My heart is free from fear.
For pine trees whisper up above
Take comfort, "God is near."

LAROES TO CATCH MEDDLERS

Abigail and Samantha could hardly wait. Christmas was just around the corner and they were getting more excited by the day. Abigail was eight and her sister, Samantha, was almost six. They had just moved into this big wooden house in Oskaloosa, Iowa, in September. One room in the house was off-limits at Christmas – the storeroom. The room wasn't heated and their mom had placed a large sign on the door which said, "Laroes to Catch Meddlers." Fear of the "Laroes" kept the two girls away for most of the month of December.

"I can't stand it, Sammy," exclaimed Abby. "I really want to see what's in that room."

"Aren't you afraid of the Laroes?"

"Yes, but this is our chance. Mom isn't home and we could sneak in and out without her knowing it."

The girls were often mistaken for twins. They both had long red braids, but Abby's eyes were green while Sammy's were blue. Since Mother had declared the storeroom off limits, they were naturally curious about what was inside the unheated room.

"Let's do it, Sammy," exclaimed Abby.

"Ok," returned Sammy. She was skeptical about being caught. Abby slowly opened the storeroom door. A blast of cold, winter air rushed out. The girls entered the room and slowly closed the door.

"No wonder it is off-limits," said the ever practical Abby.

"Wow!" exclaimed Sammy.

There was a large stack of bags and boxes from Marshall Fields and JCPenney.

"These are our Christmas presents, Sammy. Do you really want to know what we are getting?"

"But I thought Santa brought the presents?" returned Sammy.

"Well Mom helps him," said Abby. "Don't tell anyone about this," she told her little sister.

The girls cautiously left the room, closing the door quietly.

"I'm thankful that the Laroes didn't come after us, Abby."

"Me, too, Sammy."

WHAT CHRISTMAS MEANS TO ME

Oh what does Christmas mean to you?

It means a lot to me.

Not only toys and Santa Claus

And gaily lighted tree,

But somehow Christmas to my mind

Much greater thoughts convey:

Of angels singing songs of praise

That glorious Christmas day;

Of wise men coming from afar

And bearing gifts so rare;

The humble shepherds kneeling

With their heads bowed low in prayer.

But most of all I see the Babe

Asleep on fragrant hay

For he was God's great gift to me

On that first Christmas Day.

LOIS WILK

Lois Wilk was a travel agent in the Antelope Valley for thirty-four years. She has traveled to over 105 countries and has many stories and adventures to share. Her clients suggested that she needed to write a book of her experiences. Becoming a member of the Antelope Valley Writers Association has helped her to learn how to describe the world and all of its beauty, sadness, happiness, and humor.

Since retiring this past year, Lois has been hard at work putting together the amazing tales of her travels. She hopes to have them all written and compiled into a book for our reading enjoyment in 2015.

MEMORABLE MOMENTS, SOUNDS OF SILENCE

Flying into Ayers Rock in Australia, I was impressed with its size. I am not usually taken back by the size of rocks, but I was in awe looking down on it from the plane. It is called the "Big Red Heart" and covers a huge amount of territory. The 650 million-year-old sandstone formation rises over 986 feet above the surrounding terrain with an additional one and a half miles below ground. It is some five miles in circumference.

After checking into the hotel we freshened up for our unusual adventure titled, "Sounds of Silence." We were met by an old bus with the windows lowered. It drove us for no more than five minutes before we were surrounded by the "bush." All of a sudden, we stopped and were asked to get off the bus. It was desolate and we looked around and wondered what we were getting into. We were surprised to see two men and one woman dressed in tuxedo outfits and carrying champagne coming over the knoll. Smiles covered everyone's faces, with the knowledge that we were going to experience something unusual. We were invited to walk on a path towards the knoll to a table with glasses, which the waiters filled with the bubbly.

Next, we were asked to continue up the path to where a fellow was playing the didgeridoo, a wind instrument that was developed by the indigenous Australians of northern Australia around 1500 years ago and is still being used. Soon hors d'oeuvres were served. In addition to the standard fare, some of the selections were made of kangaroo and alligator, for the more adventurous travelers.

We stood on the top of the knoll to watch the sunset before heading down the other side of the hill. All of a sudden there were lights in the middle of nowhere. On one side was a buffet set up with two chefs waiting to help us with our meal. They had kerosene lamps set up amongst the food selections. Looking to the other side of the buffet, we saw tables set with lit candles. After eating a fabulous meal, we were asked to put out the candles and lamps.

There was total silence as we sat in the darkness when, a beam of light appeared. Behind the light was the guest speaker who had us look up to the brilliant southern skies with the Milky Way gleaming amongst stars and constellations. It was awesome.

Following the guide's presentation there was a loud noise and looking away from the camp we could see the headlights of the bus coming to pick us up. We were thrilled with this experience. To this day, when someone talks about Australia, the first comment from this group is, "That was the best tour we have ever had – the Sounds of Silence."

THE CAKE

At my writers group it was announced at the end of the meeting that our assignment for the next week was to write on the subject "food." What a subject! What to write about? I thought to myself, cooking is not my cup of tea or interest. I was stumped. Then I remembered an incident.

At my grandmother's farm milk was placed on top of the fruit pies for desert. My mother carried on this tradition into our home and more. Besides milk on pies we poured mmilk over the top of our slices of cake. It was yummy.

One afternoon, my youngest daughter, Janice, had a friend over for a visit. Asking her friend if she would like a piece of cake, the response was yes! Janice cut the cake and placed it on a dish, and then asked her friend if she would like some milk to go with the cake. Again, yes was her answer. Janice immediately poured milk all over the cake and her friend freaked out.

"What are you doing?" she asked.

Janice answered her back with, "You wanted milk with your cake."

Her friend answered, "I wanted milk in a glass!"

These two still laugh about it to this day (thirty years later). In fact, Janice still puts milk on her cake or pie.

I haven't added milk in years. Perhaps I ought to give it a try the next time I have my cake or pie.

HONNNIEE, HONNIEE

Sailing through Australia and New Zealand, a group of us were sharing a table with two video cameramen. They were onboard to film daily takes of the cruise. Each evening they would present what they had filmed that day to show to possible buyers at the end of the trip for a souvenir. They were young and lots of fun.

Each night I would have the Dining Room bring a celebration birthday cake to our table even though none of us were actually having a birthday. The group, including our new friends the cameramen, had a great time.

On the third evening of our nightly celebration, a woman passenger came to our table and asked why we were having daily birthday celebrations. Our response was that we all had birthdays at the same time and decided to celebrate on a cruise together. She wanted to know if we were a cult!

The next day, while we were in the city of Melbourne, we went to a bazaar and purchased some incense. Walking back to the ship, I found a stationery store where I purchased some gold star stickers.

That evening the group met in a lounge for drinks and we each placed a gold star in the middle of our foreheads. We went into the Dining Room and placed the incense in the middle of the table and lit it. The Dining Room captain was beside himself because we were stinking up the room.

One person from our group drank tea with honey. This gave us the idea to all hold hands and chant, "Honnniee, Honnnie…" The woman from the other table never came over and bothered us again.

LA RUE ALEGRIA

La Rue Alegria was born in Southern Texas, but her family has Native American roots in Oklahoma. She moved to southern California in 1952. Her husband's work on the Stealth B-2 Bomber brought her to the Antelope Valley in 1987. An avid reader as a child, she fell in love with C.S Lewis's *Chronicles of Narnia*, and always dreamt of writing. She began journaling in the early 70's, belonged to the Mystic Ink Writers group on the Internet, and was published by Poets.com.

La Rue is also an artist who has had her work on tour of the U.S. for eight years, exhibiting at Kennedy Center for the Arts, and Harvard, Princeton, Yale, and Vanderbilt Universities. She has been published in the public domain through John Wiley and Sons, New York, New York.

La Rue hopes to write and illustrate children's books as well as a write a novel and a family history/autobiography.

HERE COMES THE BRIDE

The night before my daughter's wedding it rained cats and dogs
I was so worried, the next morning the day of the event it was still
Raining, cloudy and gray
By 11:00 AM the clouds parted, the sky became clear
Five O-clock outdoor wedding, God and the Angels
Were preparing a great day for one and all

What a glorious day it had become from wet and cloudy to
Dry and clear
It was at the Ivy House
Ended up being Perfect California weather

A garden Wedding with the heady smell of Gardenias
In the garden
Everyone patiently waited a full hour
Waiting on the Bride we didn't know if she was going

To come out of hiding...
Waiting for the great grandmother to arrive
Once she was ushered to her seat
The sacred event proceeded
Here comes the Bride played loud and clear

Five generations great greats, and great, and grandmas
Dad and Mom and Bride...aunts and uncles, cousins
Best lifetime friends

Beautiful, beautiful Bride, glowing face
Long white gown with a lace Victorian collar
Pearls and sequins, it was on the cover of seventeen magazine
Embroidered daisies scattered on bodice and skirt
On netted Veil

Bridesmaids in aqua dresses with floral wreaths on their tresses
Everyone excited to hear them say, their I Do's
And tie the knot, make the big plunge, get hitched
An event everyone there remembered

The after party and reception everyone said, was the best they
Had ever attended
D.J playing up on the bandstand
Everyone who could dance proudly danced
with the Bride and Groom
Dollar dance
Her dress was covered in bills

Their destination for the Honeymoon, Grand Cayman Islands

FALL

The Brutal heat of summer is near end
Sweltering, hot burning sun hard on the skin
Moods, pets, cars, tires, just moving around
Burning hot asphalt heat, I can live without
Never have liked the summer
Fall is my beloved time of the year

Fall is just about upon us
The magical time of year
Where the trees turn
Yellow, red orange, plum, gold, brown, blazing reds

It's called Photo Synthesis
But I call it God bringing out his paint brush
To paint the towns, cities, mountains,
The woods and hills

Bathing all of nature in a Fall palette
Leaves falling, rustling down the street
Filling the gutters, knee deep in dead leaves
The sound of paper being crumbled
As children run in piles of them

Throwing them up in the air, as lite as feathers
Like trying to separate the wheat from the chaff
But all they are, are God's beautiful gifts of colorful
leaves from his trees
Cooler weather and the change of Fall is coming at last
My glorious trees are dropping their leaves of yellow and gold

Soon my dogs will be tracking them in through their doggie door
I will sweep them up never a mind, though my Gardner
won't be too pleased
His job of raking and blowing won't be done till late September,
October, Early November

I love their rustle, I love their smell, the change as they drop
From the Elms
The Oaks as well as the Maples
I long for the crisp cool nights of Fall
Arriving like an enduring lover that visits once a year

CARPE DIEM

Pluck the day
Cease it
Enjoy the pleasures of the moment
Ancestors cry out from the Grave
The great beyond
Reminded of the days they lost

Long dead Predecessors
Enjoy the pleasure of the moment
Without concern for the future
For this day this twenty-four hours
Will soon be gone and slip away

Drink in life from a Silver Cup
Sights, sounds, smells
Music, nature, beauty abounds
All around, the rainbow from mist

Things we can see and things
We cannot see with the human eye
Angelic Music all around us
Vibrations and Energy

In every corner of every room
Angelic Angels watch, lead and guide
Some of the most meaningful
Life changing experiences
Have come in a single day

By my angels who stay by my side
They are Messengers
They remind me
Carpe Diem
Cease the Day

THE ADOBE

I moved around a lot as a kid, as a result of being transplanted to California at the age of five from my grandparents' central Texas farm. My mother divorced my father and brought us three kids out to California on the train they called Old Big Red. When I was eight Mom re-married a military seaman. He was out to sea six months, home six months. He was stationed up in northern California to a sleepy little "Happy Days" town just forty miles south of San Francisco. He had gone ahead of us and rented a house. It was on Santa Rosa Street just down from the main drag of Moffat Blvd.

The house was an adobe built in the 1920's. There had been many built in that little town of Mountain View, long before the fifties. I fell in love with it, hard wood floors with a large solid wood door with triangles of beveled-edged cut glass windows. The town itself was so laid back in 1957, and after forty years I had gone back to visit it. It had not changed in all those many years other than Castro Street, which was the main drag, was lined with Asian Restaurants.

The adobe had a sweet California cactus garden, which became me and my older sister Kat's chore taking care of the garden and yard. Kat taught me about the succulents, with the mother hen and her chicks tucked so tightly around the base of the mature plant where the babies would start to grow. We had a large banana tree bearing fruit as well as grape vines bearing grapes. Just being a kid my imagination went wild, thinking Carmen Miranda would show up at any moment with a bunch of fruit on her head singing, "Eye,eye,eye,eye think you're wonderful, eye,eye,eye think you're grand!" The adobe also had a side yard with a clothes line where we hung our wash out on sunny days after the old ringer washer did its dance across the washroom floor for us one more time.

What I loved about this place, it actually had some kind of magic to it. We were all pretty happy there. There were the cherry orchards just down the road. Me and the landlady's daughter would ride our bikes to the orchards and glut ourselves with the sweet, tart cherries. We would eat our fill and then go to her house and sit out back and smash black walnuts from her old black walnut tree. We used a brick and would devour the meat from those shells like they were smoked oysters or some exotic nourishment. Sitting under the shade of the tree gave us time to talk silly girl talk and laugh.

I loved the piano window that was in the old living room, and the wonderful French style kitchen windows we sat by and ate family meals together. We never thought we would go through a hard time there. It was just too, too Happy Days for all of us. Then the Bay of Pigs conflict hit with Castro. We didn't know if our new pop would be coming back or not.

We all huddled together late one night; we said our goodbyes. I remember watching him hoist his U.S Navy gunny sack over his shoulder with his name printed on it in bold, black block letters - Arthur Leroy Williams. Smelling of old spice, clean shaven, he hugged each of us kids and Mom and said goodbye.

My sister and I would lay in the big bed we shared after tuning in the old radio to the oldie-but-goodie station. Daddy Willie, as we called him, had bought us an ancient old wooden radio in the shape of a Gothic glass window. It had a yellow cat's eye on it. Trying to tune it in was difficult, but as you got close to the station the cat's eye would glow in the dark of our bedroom like nobody's business.

With our sailor gone we were given the opportunity to do some sculpting with our landlady. She had been taking a sculpting class at the local college. Kat and I did a bust of a woman and put two fried eggs with broken yokes on it as her bust. We would get the giggles and throw ourselves back on the bed and laughing our heads off as silly sisters do.

One of the best things I liked at the old adobe was the living room hard wood floors; they were the best ever to dance on. My sister and I would get off the bus and run for the front door, almost tearing the hinges off the screen door, to see who might make it through first to turn on "American Bandstand." We would then kick aside the old faded braided rug and dance our butts off for a full hour every day except Sundays. My sister could dance like nobody's business; she could do the Stroll. The seventh step we would do the Pony, then the Swim, the Mashed Potatoes to "Hey Mr. Postman," and the Twist to Chubby Checker. It was the best time ever with my big sis growing up in the Happy Days in the old adobe.

THE STARRY HOST

I think God had us all in mind when he flung the starry host in space
It's said the beginning was a huge explosion in the Universe
The Big Bang Theory
Big Bang or not it has all amazed me

How this planet this blue orb orbits
How gravity keeps us grounded
How Oxygen keeps us alive
How trees emit Oxygen for our Planet

How our bodies are made with miles of arteries
Organs that help each other in human bodily processing
How the human brain works beyond the most complex
Computer that must be programmed by man

Even a watchmaker has a design in making a watch
Maybe the Big Bang was part and parcel of God's design
There's so much we don't understand
NASA has discovered twenty thousand
New planets within one of their lenses the size of a quarter

I wonder how many more the Hubble have spotted?
Knowing so much we still know so little
I am amazed by the creator of this world
Everyone in it, there's over six billion now
On this blue orb, that blows my mind

Houston can you hear us, do we have a read?
Houston can you hear us, do we have a read?
We're coming home...

GUARDIAN ANGEL

Pain and sorrow, Happiness and Joy
Loneliness, sweet solitude
Heartache, giggles abound
The Spirit clears my head and my thinking

I feel the caress of angel wings across my cheek
I feel a hug around my chest
It's all right I know I am not alone even when I feel so

There are angels all around me twenty-four seven
Night, morning, afternoon, they come to me during
the day, speak to me of heaven

They are there to go to bat for me, run the bases too
If I am not up to it if I am having a rough day and can't
make it through
When I lay down at night I feel a sweetness fall over my soul
Tangible like a blanket someone has thrown over me

Whispers of "it's going to be all-right" echo softly in my room
I lay my head down in sweetness, love, and peace
Dream of my Guardian Angel who stands at the foot of my bed
Anointing my feet with tears, speaking soft, sweet and low

I know I am not alone even if I should feel so, my Guardian Angel
Watches over me down here, down here on Earth below...

ERIKA HAWKINS

Erika Hawkins was born in Chicago, Illinois, and now lives in Lancaster, California. She is an avid poet and storyteller with a style all her own. She has been published with the Library of Congress, and was poet of the year with the Poetry Society. Erika has a new book on the market entitled *Aire-eeek-kah's Short Stories and Po It Tree*, published in 2014. It is a collection of her short stories and poems. She is currently working on her second book and would like to travel to London, England, this summer.

LIKE MIND

The child in me treaded a vintage of bubbles of champagne
    afloat inside a bottle.

Confined, and refined of itself to escape the scents, blows a blast
    over the land's vastness.

Flighty child's play embraces the nature of me, hunger possess us,
    revives us from universal lunacy.

Patterns resonate like a computer into ANOTHER field as
    industrious creatures labor under our feet.

Our like minds feast on the drink for the winter, and earth
    crawls like grasshoppers in the wind.

Our eyes rivet like lost balloons wading across the sky
    drunk with love.

AN ANT'S SURVIVAL

Whether or not the ant's relations were right is yet to be seen. We do know the facts, not a dream, in the mean time the situation was this. In a hiss from the snake's den, the cat hid himself of the guilt of the crime about to take place, right in the midst of night fall and dawn. A fawn would have died in its place. Out from the mitigated sidewalk from space flew down on its back a crawling, creeping ant; scurrying from a mere heavenly, righteous bird and asking in his tongue about an occasion long past. That one of his relations with no patience had ungraciously cast upon one human species.

No one knew how, why, or where, or whether to spare this little ant's life. He boxed like a cat about his past crime that went inconspicuously unnoticed. All that the cat knew was the grime within the sidewalk talked. Acting like a chicken, the mere bird balked looking both ways with no sound chirp and no one around to validate the occasion. About the crime committed of a few months past, the ant thought the questioning would not last, that he could endure the cruel and unusual punishment to the last.

The ant stood his ground on the small mound of interrogation, about his nation, as if the person of himself accused was actually abused. Someone in its place, being of another human race, set the tone for this abasement to the leg, such a bite would not heal from the bone. It was a flesh bite, with no explanation from the little innocent ant.

Now, if he were a worm, wriggling for its life, he would have used his beak, like a knife, and tore him to pieces threatening the ant. The bird stood waiting for an answer giving no indication of when he would let loose the invisible noose.

Finally, a verdict was imposed. Death, if he didn't scurry for his life. Now, the responsibility was upon the bird's shoulders. All of the boulders of the mountains seemed to resonate, falling into nature's hands. The ground shook as the bird flew to his habitat to take a look, as God was the answer.

CHICKEN SOUP

A hint of greasy white salt, and black peppered water.
Camouflaged with a chamomile bullion
in a gentleman's garden.

Ground cumin, permeated the paprika rooks' coup.
Awaiting the scream from the boil
the plucked feathers from the kitchen, caused
a curse of a stir. By design gave a sign,
that flamed under pot. Discovering clarity, profundity,
that scent strolled throughout obscure doors, under
crevices still seasoning with celery, stalked at the world's lattice.
Dignified tables, awaited to taste.

The ringing of the belled peppers, drawing, spooning away dead
spirits as the fable goes, the proof of the soup
is in the eating.

RICHARD C. ELTON, M.D.

Richard (Dick) Elton is a retired Orthopedic Surgeon who is eighty-four years young. He has lived in Lancaster since retiring from Army life in 1979. He has always had an interest in writing and plans on continuing his literary efforts until he can "write no more." Dr. Elton is proud of his son, David, an Attorney at the Trademark Office in Washington, DC., and chose to include in this anthology a treasured Father's Day letter from his son.

TIDE POOLS

The Moon is a crescent I see in the sky.
It is pleasing to look at, to behold with my eye.

Is it a fragment of Earth chipped off years ago
by a large asteroid having no place to go?

Is it there by design, regardless of cause,
for mankind to see and then give some pause.

To reflect on the fact it's because of moon's tides
there is life in tide pools and elsewhere besides.

A LIGHT IN THE SKY

As I was driving home from work in the dark of the night, I turned the radio up loud to try to experience what it was about the loudness that appealed to my teenage sons at the time. I also asked God for a sign. A light appeared in the sky which I had not seen before. Incredible, I thought, why am I doing this? It was only a short drive and when I entered the housing development where I lived I turned down the radio so as not to disturb my neighbors. I turned into my driveway feeling a bit crestfallen that I had played a silly game.

When I opened the car door and got out, I looked up into the sky and there, facing me, was an almost full moon. Yes, I felt, this was the light in the sky, but I had seen it before. But had I really "seen" it before?

I reflected that I had taken my children to see the moon rocks at a museum in San Antonio. Shortly after that historic trip to the moon, an editorial appeared saying we were all alone in the universe, giving this thought a negative tinge. The moon, he said, was just a big rock thrown there to go around the Earth and regulate the tides.

Then it struck me that if I were the Constructionist and had to solve the problem of creating tides on Earth, so there could be life on Earth (life in tidal pools is necessary for life on the dry land, so I've been told), what least expensive thing to do but to throw a rock around it. Which is what was done perhaps by an asteroid hitting the Earth many years ago.

Now I was feeling quite good to think that contrary to us being "alone in the universe," rather, the whole universe was created as it is so that people could be here on Earth to enjoy our lives. Now I felt that I had seen the moon, a light in the sky, in a different light; I had seen the moon in a way I had not seen it before.

Because of this experience and a few others like it, I have come to believe, in a scientific manner, that there is a God, that He made us, and that we will go home to him and his heaven when we end our earthly lives. What I am still working on is why God made us? I think I'll have to ask him when I go to see him.

Richard C. Elton, M.D.

THE SPEEDING TICKET

I deserved the ticket I suppose.
But where he came from God only knows.
I looked and saw him right behind me.
Oh, no, I feared he'd not be kindly.
I sidled to the right hand lane.
He sidled too. This was insane.
His lights then flashed.
My teeth then gnashed.
I pulled off the road.
What thistle had I sowed?

My new and heavy Cadillac
could cruise quite well to there and back
at speeds of eighty, ninety or one hundred.
Not heeding local laws is where I blundered.
I was late, so went a little fast
at higher speeds that did not last.

At eighty and then ninety I was clocked.
Chosen not to be ignored I felt defrocked.
The mental vestment which allowed me
to drive at speeds I should not be
was quite removed by this young cop
whose flashing lights had made me stop.

Policemen are your friends, they say.
Perhaps he did not spoil my day.
I'll be more careful when I drive
and go no more than sixty-five.
At destinations I'll arrive,
though somewhat late, yet still alive.

Policemen, I salute you.
Unto your work be true.
Pull over those who go too fast.
The number will not be too vast
when drivers do the rules abide
since from your lights they cannot hide.

THE RUMMAGE SALE

A rummage sale? A rummage sale? Set a price? By what measure?
The stuff we might just give away might be someone's treasure?

You think it might work? Said Julia to Pat.
And what a success it was after that!

Steve and his boys brought donuts and hot dogs.
James cooked the chili. Food fit for the gods!

Joan sold a chair, and a set of kitchen glasses.
These were Dick's favorites! Ah, well, time passes.

Dave and Charles brought clothing; Laurie and others brought more.
What didn't sell was given to the local Thrift Store.

George and Nancy spied two chairs of Robert and Juliana.
They bought them and clearly thought they'd had a visit from Santa.

Pat and Bob came in absentia, Reverend Nancy sold their wares.
She had help from Carol, her daughter. It is good to work in pairs.

Stuffed animals abounded, and beanie baby molls.
Two girls, Helen and Shelby, sold Polly Pocket Dolls.

George Foreman, himself, just couldn't be there.
But Diane sold his grill. Steak, anyone? Rare?

Netflix had quite a strong rival as Julia sold movies galore.
Dick gladly bought *Miss Congeniality*, a Sandra fan to the core.

For setup, take down, signs, tables and lovely balloons,
thank Roger, Michael, Charles, Andy, and Doug for their afternoons.

To all who came to our rummage sale and bought precious things,
our thanks beyond word; enjoy the pleasure your purchase brings.

The money we made was a plus but all who were there agree
that the best thing of all that day was the sharing of camaraderie

Richard C. Elton, M.D.

ODE TO THE SPIDER

I just killed a spider.
Now I feel bad.
But it shouldn't have been there.
Still, I feel sad.

They belong in a web,
in some hidden place;
not on the floor
in my office space!

A spider is made
with great intricacy.
But we hold it aloof
outside of intimacy.

Spiders do eat flies
and insect pests.
For this they get credit
but, can't be our guests.

I'm sorry Mr. Spider,
although you mean no harm,
if you crawl upon floors
you just might buy the farm.

THE JOURNAL IN MY MIND

My mind is not a journal, but a journal's in my mind.
The journal in my mind is of a certain kind.

It doesn't look like paper; there's no type or writing there.
But as for portability, there is no better fare.

My journal's always with me, always there for me to use.
It can be hard to open, standing guard there is a Muse.

This Muse is very picky, I must select the certain word
for any given space that makes my thoughts most heard.

I can peek and look around, try words out, and write them down.
But I must always look to Muse; she must not frown.

A time comes when I see Muse smile. She looks at me and winks,
as she is doing now. My work is done. It's good enough, she thinks.

FATHER'S DAY

From: David Elton
Date: June 15, 2014
To: Dad
Subject: Father's Day

Dad, Happy Father's Day!

Several years ago I asked my own children to simply write a poem for me for Father's Day instead of buying something for me. I still have the poems, and still cherish them. I was thinking of how to honor you on your special day this year, and as I wanted to give you something a little different, a little less ordinary, I decided to try to capture my feelings for you in the form of a poem. I've never thought of myself as much of a creative writer. Although writing Office actions and appellate briefs for work does require a certain amount of creativity, it's not quite the same as trying to put your personal thoughts and feelings for someone on the written page. I was drawn to the haiku style, and decided to attempt to speak to you, and to describe who you are to me and what you mean to me, using that form of poetry. I know it is technically a Japanese style with its own particular rules – and some might even argue that the idea of haiku in English doesn't really make that much sense – and is usually focused on nature, but I wanted to give it a try just the same. I wrote two, and couldn't decide which one to give to you, so I am sending both:

Dad – character, strength
Full of love, humility
The best man I know.

Fortress, towering
Tenderness, loving, humble
To be as he, Dad.

(Letter to Dr. Elton from his son, David, on Father's Day)

WILMA P. WEBSTER

Wilma Webster moved to Mexico after graduating from U.C.L.A. She stayed 15 years and studied Medicine. She spent sixteen years as an emergency physician. Wilma joined the Army Reserves and served her country in Saudi Arabia providing medical services during Desert Storm. She then switched to the Air Force, serving for eight more years in a number of countries, including England, Japan, and Panama. After leaving the military, she returned to school and earned master's degrees in HR and psychology.

During her medical career she wrote and edited a number of documents. She was editor of the "Columbia County Medical Society Medical Bulletin" from 1989-1992. In Panama, she wrote medical articles for the base newspaper, and compiled a booklet, *Wellness Wisdom*, distributed to base personnel. From 2008 to 2011 she edited the "Chai Desert News," a monthly newsletter. She is currently working on her memoirs and loves getting help from the AVWA.

DEPLOYED!

It was Wednesday, January 16, 1991, and our plane was flying over the International Date Line. For years, our field hospital had been erecting tents and putting together tent hospitals as part of regular training; now the whole unit was activated.

It was both exciting and tense! We were headed to Saudi Arabia, a country whose language I had studied many years previously. I'd long written off my major in Middle Eastern Studies as a waste of time due to a crush on an Iranian student; perhaps that learning would come in handy after all?

"Hi, Andrew. Hi, Connie. So you're coming along for the fun!" I said facetiously. There was comfort in seeing familiar faces and talking about our uncertain future. We were proud of coming through with our side of the bargain, and disdainful of those few we'd heard about who, in spite of cashing their monthly checks, found an excuse at the last minute.

The flight was smooth and spellbound. I watched as we passed over the striking White Cliffs of Dover, an important part of the British coastline which is actually composed of chalk from the remnants of skeletons of planktonic algae. We flew over Italy, France, and Sicily, and I admired how, from the air, Italy *does* look exactly like a boot ready to kick Sicily!

The plane stopped to refuel in Brussels and continued over the majestic Alps, which stretch over eight countries: Austria, Slovenia, Switzerland, Liechtenstein, Germany, France, Italy and Monaco. The Alpine borders were, of course, invisible, but soon I easily recognized Egypt with its Red Sea, and then Saudi Arabia which looked like a huge expanse of barren desert.

We landed somewhere in that desert, near Dhahran, and were driven an hour south where, on command, we put our bags down near apartment complexes originally built for Bedouins but never occupied by them. Soon we were called over for a special announcement, and were stunned to learn we were now on high alert! An attack was planned against Iraqi forces at 0300 and trouble was expected.

"Begin chemical protective gear, MOPP Level I," came the order at 0230. That's the lowest level (only the suit), but over the following hour it was escalated to MOPP IV with protective suit, gloves, gas mask and all. It was better protection but felt hot and stifling.

On command we put cots down for ourselves in an open-air parking garage. It had rained a little earlier, and rather than complain, we joked that some of us had a bed and breakfast with swimming pool included. Then sirens sounded and we could hear the roaring of planes. It was a very scary time because at first we weren't sure if the planes were hostile or friendly.--- They were ours! What a relief!

'Higher ups' decided we should go to the nearby apartment complex for cover. Indeed, that made us feel better, because with scuds coming down, outside walls give a sense of security. The scud alerts were constant, and some braver souls actually watched their descent and destruction by Patriot missiles, but I just huddled for protection. That first day there were nine scuds lobbed at us - nine scud alerts! Terrifying!

In my dairy I wrote, "We began taking physostigmine tablets last night for pretreatment against nerve agent attacks (a possible side effect of these tablets is increased urination). I haven't taken a bath for three days, and my pants are soaked with urine cause there's always a line for the bathroom and I never quite make it!"

When I began those tablets I had no idea they would wreak such havoc. On the other hand, perhaps my symptoms were only a result of the anxiety and fear from knowing I could be blown to bits, or poisoned with nerve gas at any moment. "War is definitely no fun," I wrote.

A BBC radio station said we had inflicted much damage on the enemy, with no word of casualties on our side. The 'fog of war' was definitely present, and there was so much we just didn't know. But at least I was able to find my duffel bags, A and B. Perhaps getting my stuff in order would dispel some of the chaos of that first day.

Epilog: Five months later, a TWA plane brought us back to the States, and pilots and crew showered us with confetti and said we were heroes. With our training, they knew we would act responsibly in flight, so they gave us free rein of the plane, even the pilot's cabin, and when the pilot wasn't busy, which was most of the time, we'd stop in and chat. That made us feel very special, but calling us 'heroes' was way overboard. We were only honorable men and women fulfilling our oath of allegiance.

ROCK GARDEN

It was March 21, 1991, the 8th day of Ramadan, and we'd set up a tent village in the Saudi desert. What a relief knowing Saddam Hussein wouldn't waste scuds on desert sand and forty or so reservists. We put up street signs, and I joined Nikhil and Akhila, two female Indian physicians, both majors, in a tent at the corner of Bourbon and Easy Streets.

There was a shower tent where we could line up to take showers, when available. From January to March, the problem was that it gets pretty cold at night, so the water was freezing cold, and showers felt like ice baths. Brrr!

Our mission was the medical care of enemy prisoners of war (EPW's). Although at first the International Red Cross didn't want women examining Iraqi EPW's, in the end there were so many, we had to pitch in and help. Captured Iraqi doctors, considered *detainees*, not prisoners, helped do the sick call and became our friends.

In Islamic countries, the month of Ramadan is spent fasting from dawn to dusk, a religious observance considered one of the pillars of Islam. For thirty days, they are not supposed to eat, drink, smoke, or have sex during daylight hours. After dusk it's a different story and they can enjoy everything they were denied during daylight. We had Saudi translators who helped us communicate with patients and the detainees, and they'd invite us to night-time feasts at their camp. They really did feast a lot, and although I didn't observe any behavior of a sexual nature, I danced Saudi-style with some, but heard that got them in trouble later. One of the Saudi translators actually proposed to me, hoping I'd be his second wife!

Living without modern conveniences away from loved ones was difficult and stressful. For health and weight control, I continued to run two miles every day, though my feet felt heavy trudging through sand. On my runs I met some interesting characters, such as Bedouins passing through the area, and I saw camels here and there. One friendly Bedouin lady, riding on a camel, lowered her veil to tell me how much she disliked having to use it.

While working to fill the always-needed sand bags, my friend and supervisor, Colonel Deschmukh discovered a greenish scorpion. We showed the arthropod much respect and weren't stung.

That wasn't our only scare though, because a few days later, a monitor lizard frightened the daylights out of one soldier who awoke to find it in his tent. It is said these lizards are probably more scared at such moments than the soldier was and might die of fright.

On my runs, I got in the habit of putting interesting rocks in a bag and bringing them back to the tent to make a rock garden. What a good stress-reliever that garden turned out to be! I even wrote home asking friends and family members to send plastic flowers to add to my garden so it would appear more like my beautiful garden back home in Pennsylvania.

I was starting to receive the requested plastic flowers at 'Mail Call" when, in a group meeting, Nikhil and Akhila decided to extend the cover of camouflage over our tent. I objected, saying it would obliterate the rock garden I'd worked so hard on. My fierce arguments got me nowhere, they were majors, after all, and I but a lowly captain. It seems so silly now, but I cried for a couple days over that lost rock garden.

Nikhil had previously put up a sign on our tent saying, "Mama Raju's Pita," referring to her well-known culinary abilities. At the time, I'd preferred another name for the tent, but was overruled. Now, in consideration for my hardship, they rescinded their earlier decision and let me pick another name. I took down the "Pita" sign and put up my own. Finally our tent sported a sign with a name to my liking: "Bates Motel." Trying to extend an olive branch, I added the sub-title: "Featuring Mama Raju's Pita."

Life got easier as more and more EPW's were transferred to the Saudis. April and May were hotter than earlier months; pretty soon, temperatures were reaching 120 degrees Fahrenheit daily. The camouflage extension on our tent gave us good shadow to escape the relentless sun, and we followed strict orders to drink lots of fluids to tolerate the heat. With our mission finally accomplished, in the middle of June, we left our Saudi tent village and flew home. Goodbye Bates Motel!

Today if you visit my home you may see a few dusty bouquets of plastic flowers, and if you ask about them, you'll find they're left over from my rock garden on the corner of Bourbon and Easy Streets in the middle of the Saudi desert.

LOOS AROUND THE WORLD

When I was in second grade, the school had toilets that flushed automatically and made a frightful roar. They terrified me! I knew I would be flushed away if I didn't get out of there fast. I would never, ever use the school bathroom unless they forced me.

Bathroom incidents continued to haunt me into adulthood. On the road to Mexico City I begged my husband to stop at the first gas station. It was a "really had to go" situation. "Dónde está el baño?" I asked the owner. He directed me to a building set off from the gas station, about five yards by four yards in size and so low it looked like it was built for dwarfs. There was no electric lighting, but by the light of the moon I could see six holes in the floor. By the look of things, nobody in the last year or so had actually made it all the way to a hole. I would have to be a TV gladiator to make it to a usable hole without getting my feet dirty. I had to walk hunched over because if I tried to stand up straight, I would hit my head on the roof and step in the wrong place. This was one of the few times I'd thanked my father for the clogged sinuses I inherited from him. But after five minutes in there I decided I didn't have to go after all.

Our first four years in Mexico were spent in an underdeveloped suburb of the capital that didn't have running water, but we did have an American-style toilet connected to a cesspool. We flushed it by throwing in buckets of water which were brought from two blocks up hill. Many other people in the area had similar arrangements. During my fifteen years in Mexico, I never saw another toilet as bad as the one I saw on the way to Mexico City that very first day.

Nowadays I love to travel, yet I'm one of those women who, when I have to go, I have to go. In the desert during the Gulf War it was no problem. We had military latrines in our tent village, and besides, any old sand dune would do. You just had to make sure the sand dune wasn't already occupied by somebody else. I'll never forget the time I was trying to go discretely behind a sand dune and accidentally disturbed a resting camel. They make a really loud bellowing sound, which is terrifying if you're caught unaware.

In more developed areas, I imagine I could have spent a night in jail for doing what seems natural. Just the thought terrifies me, so one of the first things I learn when I go to another country is how to ask for the bathroom. In Japan you say, "Otearaiwa doko deska?"

In France it's, "Où est la toilette?" In Arabian countries: "Wayn at-towaleet?" And in Mexico, "Dónde está el baño?" It used to cost one penny to get through the turn stile into a public bathroom, or "loo" as they call it in England, and people began saying, "I have to spend a penny" when they needed to go. Now inflation has sent the price up to 30 pence, but people still say, "Where can I spend a penny?"

In 1991 I was in Bahrain on a short break from my military duties in Saudi Arabia when I asked a man directing traffic to tell me where a toilet was: "Wayn at towaleet?" That very kind gentleman directed me to his *own home*, which was close by. Most of the women scurried out of the way when I entered, but one took me to an upstairs room which had a small (four square inches) ceramic-edged hole in the floor. I found myself alone in the room, with no toilet paper and no flush mechanism, but there was a hose coiled near the hole. I've never been much of a sharp-shooter and I'd never put my aim to such a test before but I did the best I could. It took me a few minutes to figure out what I was supposed to do. The hose was the obvious solution. I turned the faucet on, but it gushed out like a fire hydrant, getting everything wet. After turning it down, I went about washing it all down the hole and squirting myself down a little too. I left everything in order, but considerably wetter than when I entered.

I was stationed at Yokota AFB near Tokyo in 1993, and their large subway stations already had both American-style toilets and Japanese-style. Japanese tend to consider American toilets to be unclean because of the potential for contamination. I was getting pretty used to the Japanese style, but one day I went to a small subway station on the outskirts of Tokyo and asked for the bathroom in my limited Japanese: "Otearaiwa doko deska?" The attendant pointed out the way. When I got there, I saw some men in the room, so I went back to see where the women's john was. He assured me it was for both men and women. Indeed I then saw a Japanese woman enter. She looked straight ahead as she went in, paying attention only to herself. I followed, but couldn't help glancing briefly at the row of five men actively using the urinals. I did my business and walked back, but when I noticed the five men were still there, I thought, "They're probably waiting to see if I'll look again!" Red-faced, and feeling like I had been caught in the act, I exited quickly.

Although Japan is the world's second richest nation, according to the Washington Post in 1997, thirty percent of its population lived in houses not hooked up to sewer lines or septic tanks, and did not have flush toilets. Yet among the more affluent Japanese, new super-luxurious high-tech toilets are enormously popular. I read the story of one American diplomat who was at a dinner party in a Japanese home when he asked to go to the bathroom. He found a toilet so modern it looked like the cockpit of an airplane! When he finished, he stood up, to try to better understand the control panel, which had labels in Japanese, but I think it was more because he was afraid of what the contraption might do to him. He spoke Japanese, but still didn't know how to flush the thing, so he began hitting buttons. First he hit the noise button, which makes a flushing sound to mask any embarrassing noises you could be making in the john, but nothing really flushed. The next button started a blow drier, which would have dried off his bottom if he'd have stayed seated. He should have remained in his seat because when he hit the bidet button a plastic arm, shaped like a toothbrush, came out and began squirting water all over the room instead of at his butt! The embarrassed young man, who preferred to remain anonymous, spent the next thirty minutes wiping up the bathroom with a wad of toilet paper.

During my years of travel, I have done an unofficial evaluation of toilets around the world, and I am convinced that the older Japanese system, squatting over a hole in the floor, is a superior way to do our business - much more hygienic without contact with any contaminated surfaces. Definitely cleaner, it is at first hard to get used to crouching down so low. Going to the john is thus an exercise in itself and sustaining that position for any time needs fortitude and practice. It's actually similar to the 'horse-riding stance' I learned in karate classes! I am sure that if we trained our children to do it that way, they would reach middle age with greater physical stamina and suppleness. Are most Americans ready for this? No way! In fact, the super-luxurious high-tech Japanese models will probably be the way of the future. The manufacturer, Toto, aims to make the bathroom so comfortable, so relaxing, people will want to stay in there for a long, long time. And now, if you'll excuse me, I must go spend a penny.

LEMOZINE RIDDICK

Lemozine Riddick now resides in Palmdale, California, but has lived most of her life on the East Coast in New York and North Carolina. She is an outgoing church woman who enjoys telling her empowering stories about her life, hoping to help others in the process. Besides enjoying writing, she is active in her community and at the local senior center. She believes that creating a positive setting causes nothing but joy. She is a loving and caring mother and grandmother who lives and teaches respect, and enjoys everything around her.

STEPPING OUT

My husband and I moved to Brooklyn, New York, in July 1959. We had just married in January. We came to New York looking for jobs, but what we had found was a whole new life.

I was born in Gates County, North Carolina. I grew up in a family of nine people – my parents, four brothers, two sisters, and myself. I am the oldest child.

Occupying 356 square miles, Gates County, North Carolina is rich in history, and its residents are quite proud of their heritage. Up until this time, I was used to only Black and White people.

After our move to New York, it was a whole new ball game. I began to meet all different types of people. I met Jewish people, Puerto Ricans and Mexicans, people of Caribbean and African descent, and more. I got involved in community activities. I attended civic meetings, and from the different people who participated, I learned different things.

One of the things that stood out was the fact that I could do my laundry on any day. Where I am from in North Carolina, you didn't do any housework on Sunday. We went to church and came home and had dinner. And this dinner had to be prepared on Saturday. But in Brooklyn, people did everything on Sunday!

This broader perspective changed things for me. I realized it wasn't a Black or White world, but we are all in this together.

I remember getting on the bus in Brooklyn on our way to the March on Washington and seeing all of the different people riding the bus together. When we arrived in Washington D.C., it was a sea of different people coming together. It was beautiful!

Now when I look back on our move to New York, I know my husband and I stepped out on faith, but we were handsomely rewarded with a rich life for our family. It is amazing what happened in our life, the many things that happened on that journey was an everyday loving procedure. Life stretched over that walk from day to day.

We all grow along the way.

MICHELE ELISE PADILLA

Michele Padilla was born in a small town in Iowa on the Mississippi River. She knew early in her lifetime that the arts were her destiny, but she put that on hold to raise five magnificent children. Arriving in the Antelope Valley in the 1980s, she found herself fascinated with the high desert and its people. She has since been striving to develop her art skills in both pottery and writing. Michele enjoys making every day a little brighter.

TIME/LIFE

Time is Life
Life is Time
But different now my friend
For Timeless is forever
and Lifeless seems to end.

A Lifeless Time however,
(those experienced have said)
is all forgotten quickly in the Timeless life ahead.

So if some fool should ask you
TIME or LIFE which would it be?
take some TIME to answer
then answer perfectly!

There is no such thing as perfect
Just puts more on your mind,
But save some room to think about
YOUR LIFE and FINDING TIME.

BLUE MOON FRIEND

Shadowed in moon dust
tales of yesteryear illuminated only by her smile.

Majestic as the galaxy
Frivolous as a twinkling star.

Welcomed like the sun,
but arriving just once in a BLUE MOON.

DOG WALK

Dusty desert sunset

Chattering of crows

Dogs barking at absolute shadows

Joshua trees whispering ancient tales

Mountain air cooling hot pavement

The setting sun resting in preparation for tomorrow

Pitter patter of fluffy feet, appreciative paws…

and puppy dog kisses!

THAT'S MY BOY

This is a short story about a short boy. He was supposed to be; he was six. His short stature, however, was jam-packed with wonder and imagination oozing like a freshly made peanut butter and jelly sandwich. Just the flourish of skinny pieces of crepe paper acting as faux streamers on tricycles lined up in a row was enough to open his can of excitement. This led to bigger and better things.

I found him hounding me at the smallest hint of a celebration where there might be a parade. From the local shindigs in our small town, to the festivals and historic holiday parades in the city, we saw them all.

During the Christmas Parade while Santa passed by on his throne, his elves hurling candy at the crowd, he spotted a poster on the building behind us. Spurning bubble gum and tiny peppermint candies, he called me over. There was a very picturesque flowery float and bedazzling dancing horses. He sounded out the big words: ROSE – BOWL – PARADE. His eyes widened, pupils dilated, and a huge smile pulled his little lips so taut it must have hurt. No need to ask; I already knew.

Three weeks later we were camping on the streets of Pasadena. This way, he figured, we could get an up-close and personal view of the glorious entourage as it passed before us.

In the morning, brilliantly flowered floats began to appear one after the other, delighting all especially my little parade junkie. It seemed like he couldn't get enough. Bumpy streets and smothering temperatures soon began to take a toll on the glory of it all; roses and carnations not to mention an occasional orchid slid off the masterfully themed floats. Adults and children nearly tripped one another as they dodged marching bands and the dancing horses to pluck one of these flowery mementos from the pavement.

The last of the floats were passing and as my son stood steady, still mesmerized by the glory of it all, I realized he had not stopped watching long enough to pick up a precious posie. As the realization struck him, he braced himself to jump quickly as the next float approached. Its beauty was striking but alas, it was a citrus theme with oodles of oranges and a gazillion grapefruit arranged to resemble large skirts for the Citrus Queen and her court. Disappointment loomed on the horizon; what was a mother to do?

Then it happened. A plump lemon took the plunge and rolled to the curb, right in front of my son!

You can guess the rest of the story. We went home and had LEMONADE! It was the kind that not only tickles your tongue, but gives your soul a little squeeze back.

Making the best of a situation, that's my boy!

BABY BALLERINA

Fairy dust flies!

Tutu flutters!

Tiny toes twisting in an effort to point.

Hints of plié and pas de bourrée

Somehow mingle with a lovely arabesque!

Petal soft kisses blown from tiny tulip lips drift to her audience.

My Baby Ballerina, Roxy-Jane.

JOYCE SANDERSON

Joyce Sanderson lives in Lancaster, California, but grew up in Mullica Hill, New Jersey, where she always had a passion for art. After moving to southern California she began to take art classes. But it was not until she took some writing classes and listened to other writers read their work that she realized she also wanted to write. Joyce is now an active member of the AVWA and is excited to start her journey into writing poetry.

LIFE IS LOVE FULL OF REASON

Love never falls
Love never gives up
Love never fades
Never walks away

Love is joy and peace
Love stands strong
Love is agape
Love is a picture full of beauty
standing on a hill top

Love is rough
Love is like a horse
 running through the river
Love runs free like deer running wild

Don't look for love
You are love

Joyce Sanderson

IN THE MIDDLE OF A STORM

In the middle of a storm, but I'm still holding on.

Call you when the storm blows over.

Can't seem to think this storm has taken control of my soul.

Oh Lord give me strength to go through this storm.

In the middle of a storm, but I'm still holding on.

Just want to cry, in the middle of this storm.

Just want to be free, in the middle of this storm.

I'm trapped but I'm still holding on.

I'm all tied up, in the middle of a storm.

Surely this storm will pass soon.

I'm still holding on, in the middle of a storm.

In the middle of a storm

I'll always hold on.

MARILYN DALRYMPLE

Marilyn Dalrymple has lived in the Antelope Valley over forty years. She worked as a photographer and writer for twenty-five years. Marilyn has had three children's books published, and her short stories have been published in nine previous local anthologies.

She is active with the High Desert Obedience Club's "Books and Barks," program, a Therapy Dog activity that provides a dog and child friendly atmosphere, which allows students to practice the skill of reading.

She is now retired and along with continuing her writing and photography, she is endeavoring to learn the art of making handmade books and papers.

THE GREAT EQUALIZER

There wasn't much Leonardo da Vinci couldn't achieve. He had enough talent and smarts for at least ten people. Does that make you feel like you don't have much in common with this genius of the High Renaissance? Let me introduce you to the Great Equalizer – human error.

Author, Michael J. Gelb, wrote in his book, *How to Think Like Leonardo da Vinci*, a few stories about Leonardo that make the genius of the High Renaissance seem more like us and, yes, make us seem more like him.

Leonardo experienced, " . . . colossal mistakes and staggering blunders," Gelb writes, and some errors in judgment wasted huge sums of money.

For instance, can you imagine how much it must have cost to try to divert the Arno River? (The Arno River flows 150 miles to the Ligurian Sea. Its drainage basin covers 1,184 square miles.) Leonardo tried – and failed. This must have sent huge sums of lira down the river and Leonardo floundering on the shore.

Another calamity this multi-talented genius orchestrated took place when he tried to automate the kitchen of Ludovico Sforza, one of the wealthiest and most powerful princes of Renaissance Italy. Gelb relates, "Asked to preside as head chef for a major banquet for Sforza and 200 guests, Leonardo created a grand plan to make each course of the dinner a small work of art."

The innovative Leonardo built a powerful stove and a complex system of conveyor belts to move the dishes around the kitchen. He even thought to install a complicated sprinkler system in case of a fire. He did indeed put his generous talents to work. How could he miss?

Fate (or should I say Murphy's Law) stepped in, however, and made the preparation of Leonardo's fabulous dinner seem more like something you would have seen in a Three Stooges movie.

The day of the event Leonardo discovered the kitchen staff did not have the artistic talent to carve the food into miniature treasures. Not to be stopped by this minor detail, the Renaissance genius invited more than one hundred of his artist friends to do the carving.

Talented as they were, the artists were not used to working in a kitchen. The artists created true works of art from the food; the dishes were moving along on the conveyor belts. But with so many people loading food and plates onto the conveyor belts, they became overloaded and came to a horrifying halt. That's when the fire started, which set off the sprinkler system, which washed Sforza's guests' dinners and part of the kitchen out the door (and into the Arno River, probably).

Now, don't you feel more like a Leonardo da Vinci?

HELP COMES IN ALL SHAPES AND SIZES

Gypsy was a tiny, flea ridden, sorry sight when I first spotted him in a playpen at a pet store. He was the one remaining kitten from an "unexpected" litter. It seemed no one wanted the white and gray kitten, but I could tell at a glance, he was just the kind of character I liked. He looked mischievous, curious and intelligent. How could other animal lovers not have seen all these qualities in him?

I purchased him and took him home with me. Within two weeks Gypsy had made it clear to our Alaskan Malamute and English Springer Spaniel that he was in charge.

He quickly taught me that dry cat food was beneath him and only certain types of canned food would fulfill his dining requirements. Snubbing the beautiful wicker basket which was lined with a blue and pink plaid baby blanket, he chose to nap on the queen-sized bed in our guest room. His favorite spot was in the center of the sun-splashed, down-filled comforter.

I could only pet Gypsy on his terms. He definitely had an attitude and a time schedule. No petting before 4:00 P.M. Between 8:00 P.M. and 10:00 P.M. he had better be petted, or loud, demanding "meows" would fill the entire house. Absolutely no baths at any time, and combing or brushing sessions were to last no longer than two minutes - tops. His routines went like clockwork and he seemed to thoroughly enjoy the station he held at our home.

Then his schedule was thrown off. I'd been diagnosed with cancer. Doctor appointments, two surgeries, and chemotherapy treatments kept me away from him much of the time and caused chaos with his schedule. It took several months before things became normal at home and my healing process began.

Gypsy seemed to size up the situation and put a plan into action. I'd lie on the couch or in bed and Gypsy would jump up on me, landing light-as-a-feather on my chest. He'd curl up, purring like his body had the engine of a Harley Davidson. The warmth and vibrations from this rascally friend was more comforting than any medical therapy could possibly provide.

As I healed, Gypsy's visits became less frequent and slowly he retreated back to his bed in the guest room, and his regular routine. He seemed to sense that things were slowly getting back to normal.

As much as I appreciated all that the doctors and medical community had done for me, I have a special place in my heart for my little in-house healer. I will never understand how Gypsy had the wisdom to know all was not well with me, just like I can't understand how he sensed my healing was complete. I am beginning to think, however, that it is not the sun shining through the window that causes the warmth and light on the guestroom's bed, but that it emanates from the angel with an attitude that sleeps there.

ADRIANA ALEXANDER

Adriana Alexander grew up in Buffalo, New York, and she is the talented daughter of AVWA member, Patricia Alexander. She began writing poems and songs when she was five years old. Her love of writing, singing, and acting inspired her to study creative writing and theater at State University of New York at Buffalo. After college she moved to Southern California to pursue a career in the entertainment world. Adriana belongs to the Screen Actors Guild and has performed in numerous films and television. She enjoys singing her original songs and has performed with her band in Los Angeles, New York City, and Las Vegas.

Adriana recently completed her PhD in Natural Health Sciences. She writes a holistic health blog and is currently writing a book about anti-aging, and another which is a collection of her poems.

LOVE IS CONSTANT

Your Love is constant
Infinite Starlight shining
It is ancient and breathtaking.

I step inside the gateway
And follow the path you have
Lit for me with the Love
In your Heart.

Love radiates so brightly
It bends time and space
So I can see the road to You
From the farthest
edges of
the Universe.

Adriana Alexander

GLIMMERS OF YOU

Where has all the time gone?
All the time that was ours....

It has been passing through the shadows
Blanketing my heart.
It has been falling through sunbeams
As glints of special moments
Light the sky....
Showering meteor memories.
These glimmers of you
Hug my soul.

Memories dance around us as
The old Victrola plays.
Wind it up one more time for me.
Put the metal needle on the record
So we can hear our song,
While we Waltz and sing along
Before you go...

"Oh the Sun shines bright
Yes it shines so bright
I know I'll see you on the other side.
Yes the Sun shines bright
Yes it shines so bright
I know I'll see you again."

NO ONE IS EVER ALONE

Bone is Bone
Bone is the Earth
Bone is the Stars
Bone is the dust of the Universe

That settled here at the beginning of time.
And God touched it with his Spark
He twirled the dust
Like a child with a stick

As his imagination went wild
With pure Love.
He breathed Life into his Creation
His new Family
And You and I were born.

This is why no one is ever alone.

THE BROADWAY MARKET

On that chilly November afternoon the day before Thanksgiving, bundled up in our down parkas, duck boots, cozy caps, scarves and gloves, our family waddled down the driveway like fluffed penguins and piled into 'Old Mary' our vintage 1964 Thunderbird. We were on our way to the Land of Goodies. We watched the snowflakes fly by as we rolled along,…tiny silver white fairies floating from Heaven glistening in the light of a rare Autumn sunbeam,…touching down and coating the wet streets of Buffalo.

Finally we saw it - the big green lettered sign of the Broadway Market! Brimming with excitement, we hurried toward the grand entrance and climbed aboard the giant silver, food-scented escalator. Gripping the black rubber handles, my sister and I attempted to swing above the disappearing stairs, giggling away while Mom and Dad discussed their lengthy shopping list.

We descended onto the ground floor, into a cornucopia of International delights. There were meat and poultry stands, produce, seafood, bakeries, a candy counter, and restaurants. This was food heaven! We examined the fresh specialty food items featured in vintage glass coolers. We bought a bottle of the market's Famous Horseradish - perfect for a juicy roast beef on kimmelweck, the classic Buffalo sandwich. And of course we couldn't resist the delectable cannolis from the Italian bakery, which we all sampled.

After our sweet treat, we began gathering the ingredients for our feast. My sister and I were assigned the task of collecting a variety of fresh nuts in the shell, while Mom and Dad picked out yams, potatoes, bread for stuffing, and a colorful array of fresh local vegetables and fruits. Dad found exotic pomegranates and we couldn't forget the cranberries for Mom's wondrous sauce. Next we visited our favorite butcher for the pièce de résistance - a fresh twenty pound turkey. With careful evaluation my parents agreed on the perfect bird. We watched the butcher wrap our turkey in thick brown paper and knot it tightly with cord.

We had acquired the main ingredients for our Thanksgiving feast but there was still one more item I just had to see. We turned the

corner and there they were in all their molded glory - Butter Lambs!
I ran over to the display where the Butter Lambs were pasturing on
green plastic grass. There were five sizes to choose from and each
Butter Lamb came with its own pink, red, or purple neck ribbon.
"Please, please, please..can we get one?!" I pleaded. "We need butter."
Though I really couldn't imagine cutting into the little lambs and
disturbing their adorable shapes. My parents agreed we could get one
and I was awarded the task of choosing a special lamb.

   With all our fare happily in tow, we said goodbye to the
Broadway Market and headed home in 'Old Mary'. The snowflakes
became flurries and a drop in temperature had arrived with the early
darkness.

   "How about a song girls?" Dad asked. "Yes how about a song?"
Mom chimed in. So we began singing one of our holiday favorites,
"Over the river and through the woods to grandmother's house we
go..." There is nothing like singing a song with your family to warm
you up.

STEVEN BRITO

Twelve-year-old Steven Brito lives in Palmdale, California, with his grandmother who happens to be AVWA member, Wilma Webster; he stays with his mom and stepdad on weekends. He has six brothers and sisters who live in Pennsylvania and in the Philippines.

Besides being an exceptional 7th grade student at Pinecrest School, Steven holds a black belt in Tae Kwon Do, takes vocal and guitar lessons, and performs in concerts at his school playing his guitar and singing.

A few years ago Steven suffered a broken leg when he was hit by a car. While recovering, he got interested in writing. He even wrote his own book, fifty pages long, that somehow got lost. But even with his busy schedule, Steven continued to write. Encouraged by his grandmother, he entered the 2014 Palmdale "Walk On Words" annual poetry contest and won. His winning poem, featured below, is engraved in concrete at the entrance to the Palmdale Playhouse.

ONE DAY

One day you'll see the best of me,
What I can be.
Oh yes, you'll see,
While you're standing there
Staring at the concrete.
One day you'll know,
My name will blow,
And I will glow
Brighter than the sun can be,
Bigger than you'll ever think.
One day you'll see the best of me.

EKENE UGOCHUKWU

Ekene Ugochukwu is a wife and mother who lives in Lancaster, California, with her husband and five beautiful children. Originally from Nigeria, she is a talented writer, and a dedicated high school teacher at the Antelope Valley High School.

MOM AND DAUGHTER

She is your best friend.

Don't you think so, Mom?

Remember the joy you felt when first held this bundle of joy.

You both have gone through thick and thin.

So forgive and forget all her flaws.

You both miss the hugs and kisses, don't deny that.

Go find her and give her a hug and a kiss.

For no better friend shall you ever find.

AMAZING AMERICA

What can the world do without you America?
What can the oppressed do without you America?
From African to Asia, from Europe to Australia
From South America to Antarctica and back to North America
Everyone needs you America

In peacekeeping we need you
In times of sickness we need you
Yes the world needs you America
In humanitarian jobs we need you,
When there is hunger and sickness you are there to help

May God continue to bless you!
Great and noble Police Officer of the world
Ever strong and dependable America
May no evil befall this great Land of the Free
And the Home of the Brave; America

THE ORPHAN

You are blessed let no one tell you otherwise.

For your keeper does not sleep or slumber.

Your parents have embarked on a journey.

But you will someday see them again if you believe.

They have kept you in safe hands.

Lucky are you, if you remain in those safe hands.

In the Hands of God Most High,

Please be sure to remain there.

He'll provide all your needs.

You'll never lack if you believe.

Just believe then that you are blessed.

The roads may seem dark but He is ever by your side.

Fear not Dear, it is well with you.

MMELI UGOCHUKWU

Mmeli Ugochukwu, gifted young writer and daughter of Ekene Ugochukwu, has already published her first book at the age of twelve. She is now an experienced published author at the age of thirteen!

Mmeli is the first of 5 children in her family. She was born in Nigeria but moved to America with her family when she was very young. An 8th grader at Sacred Heart School in Lancaster, California, she is a talented poet and storyteller. Her book, *Jane's First Day In School: Eating Bugs*, is about moving to a new school, being bullied and finding new friends. It is available for sale on Amazon.com.

DON'T CLOSE THE BOOK

Little Girl.

Get up.

Your story is not over.

Not yet.

Do not close the book.

Turn the page.

Put the book down.

Just do not close the book.

Don't you want to know what happens next?

So much can happen if you just don't close the book.

ELECTION

Some people always incompetent

Saying vote me for president

We do as they say

Every single day..

And tomorrow too, they swing a bat

While I try to get a hat

So I try not to scowl or throw in the towel

Because I'm told it will get better

I know it gets better

It has to get better doesn't it?

AUDREY VANDENBERG

Audrey VanDenberg is a resident of Lancaster, California. She describes herself as a writer, dreamer, weaver, painter, seeker, gardener, student; and a grandmother, mother, daughter, sister, friend, neighbor; double-Aries-Leo water dragon. All in all, she jests that she is your average Southern Californian/Japanese-Dutch American.

NAMING

even if
thousands of royal butterflies name the wind
will stars abide
will turtlette mariners know
will moonshine hear their truth
for if none speak
with homeward tongue
how can they name the wind the same

I see marigold waves
fluttering over sunshine trumpets
I feel the shifting sands
beneath bare toes
kissing me with warm yellows
hugging me with foamy greens

I wonder
at tides return
even if I point toes
toward a dimly remembered
moonlit compass
leading home can I
name the wind
the same

MIKASA

O what a surprise   an Indian Feast

so *not* PC…   Two Rivers

a Teepee and a Painted Desert

A ribbon of blue water   cuts

through sandstone and stoneware

the cool shadow runs beside it   reminding me

to acknowledge   My Home is

Wherever Memory Lives   No mortal

unties the knots that bind us

No other can leave us

singular and alone   For

our floors and roofs do not contain

sweet waters of remembrance   anymore

than they banish dusty thoughts

And this is as it should be   We live with

the living and the memory of the lived

We are a continuum

a link in the delicate

chain braided into anchors' weight

We are woven

like the colors of my native sand

into sunrise   and sunset unravels the cloth

But like Penelope

we repair and re-weave and remember

our nets   our threads   our links.

Audrey VanDenberg

MS. MATA ENDLESSLY

I hear her complaints as deadbolt fumbles

I hear her cease as key finally slides

I hear her growl *bout time* as door opens

she peers outside   a nosey witchy patrol

I hear her eyes return to me

but a moment has passed

I hear her demand dinner and desert as I plead

can I just have a moment

I hear her insist *something good* this time

as I pause gathering thoughts

I hear her whine she's *been waiting all day*

for this time of complaint listing

(my tiny acknowledgement)

I hear her throughout my heard world

necessaries tended she will slumber

a furry pile of pounds in my lap

Tomorrow her courtship replays again

TRISHA PRITCHARD

Trisha Pritchard is a librarian with the Littlerock branch of the County of Los Angeles Public Library. Trisha earned her Bachelor of Arts in English and Creative Writing at CSU at San Bernardino, and her Masters in Library and Information Science at UCLA. She relocated to the Antelope Valley to start her career as Reference Librarian at the Lancaster Library. Soon she was promoted to manager of the Littlerock branch. Among her accomplishments, she created the monthly Write Is Might: a Writing Club led by Jude Bradley, a local author.

Trisha currently resides in Lancaster with her husband, son, and two dogs.

THE UNWILLING CHOICE

"Welcome to the show. We have a special guest today whose debut book, *The Unwilling Choice,* has the *New York Times* calling it 'a soon-to-be bestseller with an emotional hit to the heart' and 'best new memoir of the year.' Before we bring her out, let me read the introduction of her book:

> The words "Good things come to those who wait," and "God's Plan" should not apply to me. Yet, I don't really have a choice. There are many reasons why I should wait, and there are many reasons why I shouldn't. My head says one thing; my heart emphatically argues the opposite; and very convincingly too. So what do I do? As a compromise, my new husband says, "If it happens, it happens, but I hope it doesn't."

Please welcome Stephanie Thomas to the show. Stephanie, as you heard, I just read the first part of the introduction of your book, What made you decide to start the book using that kind of language?"

"Well, I wanted the book to be about the psychological ups and downs in dealing with infertility; the race of a women's body against time can be and is very traumatic emotionally and psychologically and

I wanted to show that I know from experience that a choice that you want to make can be taken out of your hands."

"Stephanie, let me read the rest of the introduction, then we'll talk about how you came to write this book:

> We are not talking about such dilemmas as: *should I lose my virginity to this guy?* or, *should I quit school and get a job?* In both instances, time is not an issue. You can wait a good long while to lose your virginity and you can certainly go back to school if the job doesn't work out. But, if time *is* an issue, what do you do? Fortunetellers would be a strong temptation, but they are unreliable and you certainly cannot base a life decision on the flip of a card or the glow of the crystal ball. Once, years ago, I prayed so hard and so intensely that for the first time ever, I felt a divine assurance that it would happen to me. However, circumstances have changed since then. Dare I still believe it?

Tell us about the 'circumstances' here. Why did you write this book?"

"In my life, I feel like a mule with a dangling carrot dancing in front of me, just out of my reach. Just when I think I might catch my dream, something snatches it away, and it's gone, maybe forever. You see, my first husband and I tried for eight years to have children. He had a low sperm count so we made frequent visits to an infertility clinic. I learned to keep track of my temperature and use an ovulation detector kit. As soon as the signs were right, I would notify the nurse and arrange for the artificial insemination procedure the next day. My husband would go there an hour and a half before me to masturbate into a cup and give it to the lab so they could do the count and motility check as well as prepare the 'specimen' for insemination. When I got there, I would lie on the table while a long tube that carried the sperm was inserted into my uterus. The sperm was released right at the entrance of my tubes. This experience was not the least bit romantic. My husband would sit on the couch next to the table and read a magazine. I couldn't get him to even hold my hand during the procedure."

"Why wouldn't he hold your hand? You're the one that's going through the roughest part of it."

"He was really uncomfortable about the whole situation and maybe it was his way of staying detached from it. At the time it did hurt me, but then I thought that the end justifies the means."

"Hmm, I don't know. If it was me, I would be right there going 'what're you doing now?' and always be in the doctor's face making sure everything was done correctly. Not only that . . .hey, I'm serious . . . not only that, but I'd be right at my wife's ear whispering sweet-nothings just to, you know, at least act like we're in a romantic situation. . . . However, that wasn't what happened, right Stephanie? So then what did you do?"

"We finally decided to go with the recommendation of my doctor and have the fertility shots; the kind that have been known to produce quintuplets and the likes. The out-of-pocket expense is considerably greater, and the insurance at first refused to authorize the procedure."

"What happened when the insurance refused authorization?"

"I wonder now if it was divine intervention, because it was then that I really looked at my relationship with my husband and found it lacking considerably. I spent years trying to get pregnant so I could have a child when all along I had one already. There had been many signs throughout our eleven-year marriage that I had disregarded, thinking that he would change once he had the responsibility of a child. I would have found out the hard way. Once I made my decision, I called the nurse to inform her that we were dissolving the marriage and would no longer need fertility treatments. Ironically, she told me that the insurance authorization had just come in that day."

"But didn't you love your husband? I mean . . . you must have to even consider having a child with him."

"I did love him. He was my first love and when I married him, it was to be forever . . . but the man I married never grew up. I realized that early in our marriage when he nearly bankrupted us with his gambling habits. After that, there were many such problems that we had as a result of his immaturity. I guess I just blocked out the fact that it was killing my love for him. When I thought of divorce, believe me, I fought it. I didn't want to be another statistic. But I realized that it was right for me and, whether he acknowledged it or not, for my husband. I grieved the death of the marriage for a long time. And it is a death; you have to grieve and work through the pain before you can move on with your life."

"What has happened since your divorce?"

"Well, at thirty-two years of age, I started my life over. I decided to go back to school and work on getting a degree in a field that has always interested me, Creative Writing. I love to read books of all kinds, they inspire the creative side of me and I wanted to write as well as edit other people's creations. But, in fulfilling this dream, had I sacrificed the other? I am thirty-five years old now, by the time I get my master's degree I will be almost thirty-eight. My new husband of eleven months wants us to wait until I graduate and get a job as an editor before getting pregnant."

"Why? If it is important to you, why doesn't he want to have children now?"

"His reasons are very valid. He made bad decisions some years ago and is now spiritually stronger for it. He is forty-four years old. He is grateful for the job he has now, however, we are relying on my student loans to stay afloat. Plus, his job doesn't offer any kind of retirement plan or benefits. He is depending on me to get a job that does. We are not financially able to care for a baby right now. In my first marriage, I was planning to be a stay-at-home mom. Now that my life has changed drastically and I am in a give-and-take marriage, I will be the breadwinner and he will be 'Mr. Mom'."

"Why did you decide to remarry?"

"I met my new husband while working nights at a bar. He was the bouncer there and we got to know each other really well over a couple years. Eventually, we realized that we were in love. He is so different from my last husband. For the first time, I now know what it feels like to be taken care of by a man. To love him and care for him as he does for me is a great joy in my life."

"So now you plan to work and he will be the stay-at-home dad, but you will have to wait a few more years. How does that make you feel?"

"I am not getting any younger and neither are my eggs. A man produces millions of viable sperm every ninety days. A woman does not have that luxury. She is born with the eggs already in her ovaries. The threat of Down's Syndrome and other such defects are greater after the age of thirty-five."

"Statistics are showing that women are waiting longer to have their children."

"I know, but at what cost? My husband has a sixteen-year-old daughter from his first marriage, and she lives with her mother and stepfather. No matter how much he loves me, he would never be able to understand what I went through and what I am still going through. He *has* a child, so it would not make any difference to him if he does not have another. By the time we get ready to have a child, his daughter may have a baby of her own, making my husband a grandfather."

"Members of our studio audience will find a copy of Stephanie's book, *The Unwilling Choice*, under their seats. I'd like to read a poem that she wrote in the chapter titled, 'You Against the World.'

DON'T TALK TO ME ABOUT IT

Don't talk to me about the plus sign or the first pelvic exam
Don't talk to me about the nausea or pickles and ice cream
Don't talk to me about that first picture or the heartbeat
Don't talk to me about that first flutter or that first kick
Don't talk to me about pounds and maternity clothes
Don't talk to me about swollen ankles or back pains
Don't talk to me about the pains of labor or the Epidural
Don't talk to me about the miracle of birth or ten perfect fingers
Don't talk to me about milk filled breasts and embarrassing leaks

Don't tell me any of this, but most of all -
Don't talk to me about how lucky I am - spared from all of this
Because I don't want to hear it!

Let me tell you about a new death every 28 days
Let me tell you about the tender, swelled breasts
And the microscopic sensation of conception,
Only to find it was my heart and brain that conceived deception
Let me tell you about the names that would never be,
Dozens that I won't have to choose
Let me tell you about delivery methods, all carefully researched
Lamaze, under water, suspension, and my favorite - hypnosis
None will ever be used, not by me, anyway
Let me tell you about having a numbered stranger injected in me
Frozen after collection, then thawed for injection
Let me tell you about the Basal Chart – 10th of degrees measured
And the "kit" - it tells you when to be loved
By the long thin tube in the privacy of your own doctor's office

So don't talk to me about watching your "brats" anytime I want
Because, I know that you don't envy me
And I won't say how lucky you are to be spared my experiences
Because I know you don't want to hear it!

I can see that many of you in our audience are affected by this poem. Stephanie, I wanted to ask you about the last line in your introduction, 'dare I still believe it?' After all the emotional turmoil you've been through, how would you answer that question now?"

"Every time I see a pregnant woman, a baby, or young children I start to cry. Especially hard is hearing about the situations that large families find when faced with yet another pregnancy or worse yet, a teen mother dumping her baby in a trash bin. Why do these things happen? Why is it that the people who desperately want children find that they cannot have them, and why are there people who constantly have them when they are clearly not wanted? My husband says that God has a plan for everyone, and since we have not used any form of birth control for nine months, God's plan must mean that it is just not yet meant to be. So yes, I dare to believe."

"Thank you, Stephanie, for sharing your experience with us. We are going to take a break and when we come back we will meet another aspiring author, he came from an unusual . . ."

Stephanie walked into the bathroom after switching the TV off. So much has happened since I taped that show, she thought.

She and her husband spent a month at a mountain retreat. There they communed with nature, God, and each other. They returned home spiritually rejuvenated. Stephanie realized that their lives were in the hands of God and she learned to appreciate her husband's love for her in a whole new dimension. If God meant for them to be childless, that was okay. He gave them each other; and Stephanie meant to make every moment count. It was two months before Stephanie realized that she had not had a period for awhile.

The stick that was the pregnancy test rested on the bathroom sink waiting for the appointed time to be read. Stephanie thought about her life. She had two more years of school. Yet, she had never felt more blessed or happy. Her life was with her husband and nothing was going to change that - nothing. "Thy will be done," she whispered. Stephanie looked at the stick.

KIT BENNETT

Kit Bennett is a transplant to Palmdale, California. Originally from a Wisconsin farm, she has lived in various places in the Los Angeles area for almost ten years. Her acting career has taken a backseat as she works on multiple ways to restore her health. A six year battle with chronic Lyme disease; co-infections, and toxic mold poisoning have been a life threatening detour of struggling, learning, and great personal growth. Kit does not consider herself an author at all and can only write when she is truly moved and inspired. She is married and is the proud mother of two basset hounds, Maggie Mae Flower and MonaBelle Clementine Howler. She enjoys volunteering at Basset Rescue Network in Acton and works to spread awareness of tick borne diseases in whatever capacity she can.

SIGNIFICANCE OF A STRANGER'S SMILE

Today marks the first time I got out of the house since my central line surgery. This procedure slices thru your jugular vein and leaves a catheter in your heart for the delivery of long term IV antibiotics or chemotherapy drugs. I have difficulty lifting my head from lying down and I can't move my head from side to side yet.

The catheter is itchy and it feels bothersome to have clothing on top of it, so I spent today doing something I never thought I would do with my mom. We went shopping for low cut shirts together. When I was a teenager, my mother was the Nazi of modest dressing. I wouldn't dare leave the house wearing anything that could be perceived as provocative. I am now thirty-six years old, and my mother's voice still lives in my head and resonates with disapproval every time I look in the mirror.

"You're not going out looking like THAT, are you?"

We found several scooped neck shirts with soft fabric that not only feature my cleavage but also completely bypass the tube coming out of my chest, so not only will I be showing off my boobs, I will also show off my hard-wiring. Lovely! I'm really going to turn heads with this new look.

I teased my mom and told her I never thought we would ever share this experience with each other. She told me that now I was older and married; I could wear whatever I wanted. OMG! Wardrobe approval from my mother. Never thought that would happen. I almost keeled over in the handicapped dressing room.

It has been very interesting watching how people react to me. I thought the sight of me would scare children and they would run screaming to their mothers, but kids didn't notice me at all. Of course their line of vision is between my knees and butt, not on my chest. Men, for the most part, are in their own little universe and don't notice the blood soaked bandage and wiring coming out of my chest either. I can think of only one exception who was gawking at me.

The women are 50/50. Half of them either don't notice or do a believable job of being polite, and the other half look at me like I am some kind of circus freak. Their eyes will become fixated on my hard-wiring and their mouths will hang open. Or, they will put on their sunglasses indoors and continue gawking at me. Um...hello? I'm not blind; I can still SEE you staring at me thru your sunglasses. How rude! I found the best way to deal with this tacky behavior is to stare right back at them. They quickly avert their eyes once they notice I am on to them. It usually doesn't take long.

I don't mind if people ask me questions, because it is a great opportunity to spread awareness about Chronic Lyme, a very misdiagnosed and misunderstood disease, but I do mind being gawked at.

I would like to close by commenting about a random stranger's smile and what it meant to me. After feeling so self-conscious about the foreign object sticking out of my chest and having so many women gawking at me, I saw a man passing with his two preteen daughters. He just looked into my eyes and smiled. It was as if this random stranger just saw me for who I was inside versus what I looked like on the outside. I smiled back at him and he just made my day. I still think about that random act of kindness.

So maybe when you're out and about, and you see someone who looks different, don't stop and stare; just smile at them. You have no idea how good it will make them feel or what a difference it could make.

KATHY ANDREWS

A native Californian, Kathy Andrews has lived in the Antelope Valley for eleven years, during which she found herself transformed into a true Desert Rat. She and her husband can rarely resist the lure of the open road, and they get out to explore as often as they can. Dabbling in genealogy and compiling family histories sparked an interest in creative writing, a hobby she finds most entertaining. Semi-retired, Kathy works in her husband's financial services practice.

MOJAVE DESERT MAGIC

Have you ever stood in the silence of the desert only to realize
that you were hearing the melody of a desert wind?

Have you felt a desert heat so hot that it takes your breath away?

Have you ever stood on a lofty perch
and gazed across a seemingly empty valley
and marveled to realize that you could see for a hundred miles;
your view dotted only by sand, sage, ancient creosote
and stands of junipers and stately Joshua trees?

Have you bounced along in your vehicle on a sandy, rock strewn,
two-rutted road across an endless landscape of muted colors;
soft sage greens, velvety tan and beige, every hue of brown
and the mauves and purples of the mountains at dusk?

Have you traveled past places where once upon a time
men wrested gold and silver from the earth;
where now remains only weathered and crumbling
timbers and stones to mark the site?

Have you witnessed the drama of a desert sunset
where impossibly blue and immense skies
melt into hues of stunning pinks, oranges and fiery reds;
forming the backdrop for perfect ink black silhouettes
of the hills and mountains?

Have your eyes followed the line of an old barbed wire fence
into the distance until it vanishes from view;
a vestige of a vintage cattle ranch;
or perhaps still encircling a distant ranging herd?

Have you ever wandered the streets of a desert ghost town;
tracing the steps of its former inhabitants;
imaging as you beheld the empty weather-beaten dwellings,
the glory days of those long ago towns
and the folks who called them home?

Have you ever stood in an ocean of fiery orange poppies,
or feasted on the wildflower rainbows of a desert springtime?

Have you ever walked a desert path and startled a gangly jackrabbit,
or a covey of quail or lightening fast lizards from their hiding places?

Have you ever sat beneath a desert night sky of a million stars
and been caressed by the warmest evening breeze,
and perhaps as you gazed up,
been startled by the streak of a shooting star
across the infinite blackness?

Have majestic canyon walls of red rock and fantastical formations,
carved by water and wind over the eons
risen up around you as you passed through their portals
and descended into their depths?

Have you stepped back in time in the presence of
ancient petroglyphs and pictographs carved
and painted into stone
hundreds of years ago by a vanished people?

Has the solitude and vastness humbled you
and perhaps stirred your spirit
at the imposing splendor of it?

Tamed yet still wild, brutal yet beautiful, immense and magical
ancient and enduring
each of these pieces meld together to form
the natural and historic mosaic that is
The Great Mojave Desert.

Civilization gnaws at the edges of the great desert
yet at its heart it remains a place of desolate beauty,
of exhilarating vastness
where adventurous souls may still experience
a tast of the Wild West and
the unique grandeur that is the desert.

OLEG KAGAN

Oleg Kagan is a writer and librarian. He currently manages the Topanga Library for the County of Los Angeles Public Library system. His prose and poetry have appeared in several anthologies including Rokoko, Saturation, Ohmanut, Westwind, Phantom Seeds, and his Haiku in others, including the Southern California Haiku Study Group yearly anthologies and the AVWA *Soaring* anthology.

Though Oleg is not an Antelope Valley resident, the AVWA considers him an honorary member as he originally founded the writers group during his employment at the Lancaster Library. Originally from Kyiv, Ukraine, he lives with his wife Ashley in the Mar Vista neighborhood of Los Angeles, California. His many talents can be viewed on his blog, lifeinoleg.com.

---

4 HAIKU

thoughts of Chernobyl
in my mouth
a metal tongue

after the blizzard
the blur of something
in the pool

garden wedding
the flower girl
feeding the koi

they all ask
about our future kids
pomegranate seeds

SMALL HOUSEHOLD PET

A ceramic duck, maybe
or the click of a glasses case closing,
a nail hitting the floor
after the clippers join,
or the squeak of an inhale
through a dry,
stuffy nose.

IN THE MUSEUM COURTYARD

Sitting next to the "Dwelling for Imaginary Civilization of Little People" in the courtyard of the New Mexico Museum of Art, I can't help but watch the sky. It is bright and blue with clouds crawling through the afternoon.

In front of me is the "Mountain Fountain" -- a nine foot high pyramid of Dakota granite. Water bubbles out of the top, taking the long way down until it disappears into the blocks at the fountain's base.

A tiny sparrow is down there. I can't tell whether it's praying or drinking. The sparrow flits to the fountain-top. I photograph it beating its wings. Moving to the other side. Bowing its head. Bowing its head. Another sparrow appears. I get them together. They bow. They drink. They're gone.

The sparrows are darting in and out of the courtyard's exterior corridor. Closing my eyes, I listen to them play.

early spring --
each sparrow moment
its own floating world

DOREEN KENNEDY

Doreen Kennedy moved with her family to Palmdale, California, from Atlanta, Georgia, about three years ago. At first it was quite an adjustment, as she looked for a way to meet people who had the same interests. She found the perfect outlet in the Antelope Valley Writers group, now the AVWA. Since joining the group, it has grown from several members to thirty. She compiled and published the group's two anthologies, *Soaring* and *AMAZING*, and had the AVWA use the funds from sales of these books to sponsor scholarships through the Antelope Valley College Foundation. In 2015 she will start a new writers group just for teens.

Doreen considers education as the key to a successful life. As a teen she would not have been able to attend college without someone's gift of a scholarship. She majored in Math which led to a twenty-five year career as a technical writer. Later in her life, she returned to college and received her degree in English, Secondary Education, with a minor in Professional Writing. Her goal is to get everyone, young and old, to write and enjoy it.

LIFE DEBT

I first met my best friend at lunch. We ate outside. Not at some trendy sidewalk café with bistro sets scattered about, a dainty flower on each table. It was a factory, a shabby warehouse of a building set back off a rural business route. A noisy, dirty aberration of concrete blocks hastily assembled in once pristine woods. A section of trees had been cleared and asphalt poured for a parking lot between the building and a large creek. At least they left the creek alone. It flowed uninterrupted despite the construction, meandering through the woods and around the back of the building, and only the owner and his foremen knew what ended up in the water when no one was around to see.

Lunch was brown-bagged. There were no stores or restaurants nearby. Anyway, we were on a budget, Jerry and I, and we ate in the parking lot in his old clunker of a car, mainly to escape the noise and filth of the grease-soaked machine shop where we both worked.

"I can't take it here much longer," I repeated for the hundredth time this year. "We both need to go back to school and get out of this cesspool - find healthy, professional jobs."

"And who's going to pay the bills while we return to studentland?" Jerry would always reply. "You don't appreciate how lucky we are that Mr. Wilson gave us these jobs."

"Yeah, great jobs. You have to wear headphones to keep from losing your hearing, while the rest of your body is sprayed with oil and chemicals. And I have to listen to a lot of filthy language that wouldn't be proper in a raunchy bar. We can do better than this, Jerry. You should be designing those machines, not running them."

"I can handle it for now. And you have a clean job in the office with Annie, so stop complaining…"

"Shhhhh! Did you hear that?" I asked trying to cover Jerry's mouth.

"I hear your chewing and complaining, that's all."

"Shhh. Listen…"

The sound was faint, but distinct, and it was close by. We looked around to see if something hurt had wandered out of the woods.

"Hey, I think it's coming from the car." We both got out and Jerry walked around the perimeter; he opened the trunk - nothing there.

"No, listen… it's under the fender." And with that I dropped to my knees.

"Whoa! Wait just a minute. Let me get a flashlight before you go shoving your arm in there."

Too late. I had already reached my hand above the front tire, ignoring the pain as I pulled out a clawing, hissing, white kitten with the biggest blue eyes I'd ever seen on any animal or human being. The little fur ball was just skin and bone and eyes.

"The poor thing. It's starving." I held the creature to my chest and it immediately calmed from the warmth of my body. As I stroked its head I felt it shaking, not from cold or fear, but from contentment. That kitten was purring pure happiness.

"You know people dump their animals in these woods all the time. The strays have baby strays and they wander around until they get killed or eaten. If they manage to live they are sick and diseased. Ever hear of rabies?" Jerry's tone was so callous that I shot him a look that wavered between disbelief and anger.

"And your point is?" I asked, as I brought the kitten into our car and broke off tiny bits of meat from my sandwich. The poor thing was so hungry that it bit right down to my fingers. I already had what looked like a red tic-tac-toe grid scratched into my right arm, and until Jerry mentioned rabies, the thought hadn't occurred to me. But I continued to feed the kitten and it continued to eat.

At my insistence, Jerry searched the woods near the parking lot for more kittens. "If someone dumped a litter here, that little guy is the only survivor. Now what do we do with it?"

"Don't think too hard, sweetie, because I'm keeping him, or her." It was such a tiny thing that it was difficult to tell.

"Well you'd better figure out how to hide it for the afternoon. There are guys in the shop who take sadistic pleasure in drowning strays in the creek, and they do this with the owner's blessing."

Jerry's words only fueled my hatred for this place. We were newlyweds - young, stupid twenty-year-olds who quit college to start a life together on our own. Both of our families were against it. We weren't exactly ready for marriage either. But they didn't want us together. Jerry's parents threatened to stop his school payments unless he agreed to transfer to another college. I was on scholarship and couldn't possibly move with him. So their attempts to separate us actually backfired and forced us into our current matrimonial bliss.

We soon discovered love was free but living required money. And life without a college degree meant menial, minimum wage jobs. Jerry and I prided ourselves on being self-sufficient and would never have accepted money from either of our families. Not a penny. But we did need jobs, and Jerry had a friend whose uncle was hiring workers for a new factory. He paid more than minimum wage plus lots of overtime. It paid the bills.

But the work was hard, conditions awful, the shop crew all males, and some of the men were crude and ignorant. They saw nothing wrong with dumping waste and chemicals in the creek - as well as drowning helpless animals. No way was I going to let those creeps get to this kitten. I sneaked it in the office side door where Annie and I worked. Annie was the only other female employee. She was close to retiring at a textile factory when she was laid off. Like Jerry and me, desperation led her here. I liked Annie. She was down-to-earth, good, honest people and she reminded me daily that I should leave before I ended up like her. Annie found a box that it couldn't climb out of and we hid the kitten in our bathroom, hoping that the factory noise would cover up its constant crying.

Only thirty minutes until quitting time when Henri wandered in. He was a machinist and the worst of the creeps. An annoying French Canadian fellow, a short chubby man who thought the ladies drooled over him because he spoke with an accent. As usual, he harassed Annie and me with his disgusting tales of female conquests. I tried to erase thoughts of his grimy hands touching any woman, while I prayed he would not hear the kitten over his incessant bragging.

"Eh? What is zat sound?" Henri actually stopped talking to look around the room.

"What sound? Annie did you hear anything?"

"Zat sound. It come from over zare."

To my horror, Henri opened the bathroom door and dragged out the box. He grabbed the little blue-eyed kitty by the neck and dangled it high.

"Is a rat!" he yelled. And that kitten promptly bit him. "Damn rat!" he let it go and I nearly fell off my chair to snatch the hissing bundle from hitting the floor. "I take zat rat and toss it in ze creek!"

I leaned right into Henri's face, *tête-à-tête* as the French say. "You do that," I warned him, "and your nights of passion are over – permanently!"

"Bitch! I tell ze boss what you say to me. He no want strays around ze plant. He tell Henri to kill zem."

"Well you go tell the boss . . . and tell him I said that you're both assholes!"

Henri couldn't run fast enough toward Mr. Wilson's office.

"If only he'd move that fast when he's working," laughed Annie, "quick, get out of here with the rat. I'll cover for you."

And with that I wrapped the frightened kitten in my sweater and locked us both in the car. I was done for the day and maybe for good. Fine with me. I just hoped if Wilson fired me he would still keep Jerry.

Fifteen minutes later the car door opened. "I've been looking all over for you. What's going on?"

I told Jerry about Henri finding the kitten and how we hid in the car so he wouldn't kill it. "I am SO going to tell the authorities what goes on in this place."

"No!" Jerry commanded. "Let it be. Henri has the boss's ear. Besides, Wilson probably paid someone good money to build this factory way out here and right next to the creek. Someone will just get a big bonus and we'll be unemployed."

"You know, Jerry, you used to have ethics. What's happened to you?"

"Life. Life has happened. And its cousin, Reality."

"Okay," I conceded. "But all the more reason we need to get out of this place. It is so bad for us."

"Well I have a bad feeling about this day, and about that cat." Jerry had no idea just how true his premonition was.

On the ride home the scared baby calmed down and fell asleep in my lap. "I'm naming it Blue, like those big beautiful eyes."

And that is how I acquired my first cat, and best friend ever.

Soon little Blue turned into big Blue, a large male who appeared to be the offspring of a Siamese that went slumming with a tan striped alley cat. The product was this gorgeous white cat with a light brown dusting on his ears and tail. A hint of tan striping on his legs became more visible as he grew, giving him the appearance of a miniature white tiger. And he was as fierce as one.

For whatever reason, perhaps his early encounter with Henri, Blue disliked males, and that included Jerry. If we tried to snuggle, Blue would jump up and bite him on the arm - just sink his teeth in - and then finish the attack with a low growl. So naturally, he was banned from our bedroom, and Jerry soon began to wish he had let Henri drown the animal.

But he was my cat, and I loved him. It's like Blue knew that I saved his life and now he owed me his unconditional love. A life debt, they call it in some cultures.

Blue soon claimed the highest spot in our apartment, the top of the dining room hutch, where he would perch like a lion on a ledge watching everyone and everything. Despite my efforts to domesticate him, he would never lose that wildness. His favorite activity was stalking through the high grass in the fields behind our building. He played Bengal tiger roaming the grasslands of India. To my dismay he made great sport of catching the small wild creatures that lived in those fields. Until Blue, I never knew that rabbits could scream.

Blue stayed with me no matter what. He even helped me to survive through my divorce from Jerry. No, it was not because of the cat. But Blue did open my eyes to a world outside of that awful factory. Because of him I found the nerve to quit, found another job in a clean office building. I didn't make as much money, but it was closer to our apartment and there was opportunity for education and advancement. I think Jerry was actually jealous. Despite displeasure with my reduced paycheck, he soon followed suit and quit, then decided to go back to college. He also found another job, but it was an internship that wouldn't pay much until he got his degree.

Separate work places meant the added expense of a second car. That plus no more overtime pay meant financial cuts. But I was the only one making sacrifices. Jerry took the newer car while I drove the old clunker. His only contribution to our money shortage was to suggest we get rid of the cat. "I'll cut as many corners as I have to, but I will not part with Blue," I told him.

Jerry's spendthrift habits and late hours at the office started to annoy me. But I let it go, since he was working so hard to make things better for us. It was when he didn't come home at all that I realized what Blue already knew - he was seeing another woman. Had been seeing her for a while. I truly believe that Blue could smell her on him, and that was the reason for his biting episodes.

It was over, and Blue was all I had to show from two years of marriage. I was fortunate that I still had my best friend. We moved to a small rental, a rundown duplex with expensive electric heating. But there were separate thermostats in each room. I would shut off the heat except in the bedroom, and cuddle with my cat to stay warm. Furniture was a mattress on the floor. I kept my clothes in cardboard boxes, and ate on a shelf from the closet that I propped up on two cinder blocks. But I had my freedom, my dignity, and my friend. Blue was my faithful companion through it all. Eventually we acquired furniture, a piece at a time, and I finally saved enough money to get us into a new apartment complex.

Being a single woman, I felt safer on the third floor. The living room had a big picture window with a ledge providing a high vantage point that Blue loved. But the downstairs security door made it difficult at first for him to get outside. Blue always had that wild streak in him, so he would not stay indoors. But cats are smart, and Blue was exceptionally so. I would take him downstairs and let him out, and when he was ready, he would come back to the big security door until I, or someone else, let him back in. Everyone in the building got to know him, so that was never a problem.

The problem was my neighbor down the hall. He complained that Blue was urinating on his doormat. I didn't believe him until I saw it with my own eyes. Blue would strut down the hallway and wiz right on this guy's door mat. How strange? Was it an all out hatred of men, was he marking his territory, or like with Jerry, was Blue trying to tell me something.

"Blue, how will I ever meet a nice man if you keep biting them and peeing on them."

It snowed one evening. It would be a record snowfall. I had promised my sister that I would come over for dinner. My defoggers on the clunker didn't work, as usual, so I had the windows open to see where I was going. Blue was curled up in a blanket on the back seat when my tires went into a skid. I overcorrected and the clunker flipped off the road and down an embankment. It ended up on its side, in a creek bed, driver's side down. I couldn't get out. I lay there thinking of dumb things, like eating snow until someone found us. At least I had Blue to keep me from panicking. Suddenly Blue jumped up on the steering wheel and the horn blared. "Yes, the horn! And thank goodness you're okay, pal." And that's when I discovered I wasn't. My left arm was pinned and my right arm was broken. Meanwhile Blue managed to climb up the passenger side and was digging his way through the snow that had piled on the partly open window. He began to dig like a cat in a litter box. Maybe he has to go, I thought. "We can't panic now cat. Come back and hit the horn." But he kept digging until he pushed his big cat head up through the snow. He had made enough of a hole to squeeze through with his strong feline body and escape from our frozen prison. "Go ahead, get out of here. Save yourself, you were always a survivor." And with that his tiger tail disappeared through the hole. I imagined him leaping through snow drifts, nothing but big blue eyes. My pain was incredible, but I took it as a good sign that I could still feel my legs.

"You know," said the strange man as he covered me with blankets, "I would have never looked down here were it not for that cat. At first I thought it was a baby tiger leaping across the road -

almost hit it. Got out to see if it was okay. It just sat on that big rock on the side of the road, staring at me with these incredible eyes. But when I got close it took off down the hill. That's when I noticed something blue below, same color as those cat eyes. Realized it was a car."

When the rescue crews arrived, Blue had vanished.

Somehow he found his way home to the apartment building. As usual, someone let him in and he went straight upstairs, peed on my neighbor's doormat, then curled up at my door. The neighbor was heading down the hallway to once more complain when he saw Blue and wondered why I hadn't let him in. And that's when he noticed the trickle of blood on his mouth.

"She would never go away and leave you like this."

My neighbor was shocked when Blue actually allowed him to wrap him in a blanket and take him to a nearby animal hospital. The next morning he knew why as he read about the dramatic rescue of a woman whose car went off the road and was buried in the snow. And about the tiger cat with the big blue eyes that saved her and was now missing. She had broken ribs, a broken arm, and a concussion, but was going to be okay.

Blue's jaw was broken. He got kind of scrawny from the liquid diet, but he stayed with Peter, my neighbor, until I was out of the hospital. Not once did he bite the man, and he never again peed on his doormat. I couldn't thank Peter enough for taking care of Blue, and not long after, he was also taking care of me. Life debt – paid.

INDIVIDUAL COPYRIGHTS

The following are Copyright by STEVE ORDWAY

© 2014 Sitting on Go – Life at the Fire Factory

© 2014 Close Call

© 2014 Chihuahua

© 2014 Happy Chief

The following are Copyright by ELAINE BROWN

© 2014 Silver Queen

© 2014 Ice Fantasy

© 2014 Rose Garden

© 2014 Moonlit Garden

© 2014 Summers in Canada

© 2014 The Spirit of Kauai

The following are Copyright by MELINDA M. HUNTER

© 2014 Rain

© 2014 Spring

© 2014 October's Voice

© 2014 Laroes to Catch Meddlers

© 2014 What Christmas Means to Me

The following are Copyright by LOIS WILK

© 2014 Memorable Moments, Sounds of Silence

© 2014 The Cake

© 2014 Honnniee, Honniee

The following are Copyright by LA RUE ALEGRIA

© 2014 Here Comes the Bride

© 2014 Fall

© 2014 Carpe Diem

© 2013 The Adobe

© 2014 The Starry Host

© 2005 Guardian Angel

The following are Copyright by ERIKA HAWKINS

© 2014 Like Mind

© 2014 An Ant's Survival

© 2014 Chicken Soup

The following are Copyright by RICHARD C. ELTON, M.D.

© 2014 Tide Pools

© 2014 A Light in the Sky

© 2014 The Speeding Ticket

© 2014 The Rummage Sale

© 2014 Ode to the Spider

© 2014 The Journal in My Mind

© 2014 Father's Day

THE END

www.ingramcontent.com/pod-product-compliance
Lightning Source LLC
Chambersburg PA
CBHW031346170626
46807CB00002B/859